Books by Richard Mitchell

THE LEANING TOWER
OF BABEL and Other Affronts
by the Underground Grammarian

THE LEANING TOWER OF BABEL and Other Affronts by the Underground Grammarian

RICHARD MITCHELL

with an introduction by

THOMAS H. MIDDLETON

Let us affront and reprimand the
smooth mediocrity and squalid
contentment of the times . . .

— Ralph Waldo Emerson

LITTLE, BROWN AND COMPANY · BOSTON · TORONTO

FIRST EDITION

All of these pieces have appeared in
THE UNDERGROUND GRAMMARIAN.

Illustration on p. 218 by George Herriman from *the lives and times of archy and mehitabel* by don marquis. Copyright 1930, 1933 by Doubleday & Company, Inc. Reprinted by permission of the publisher.

LIBRARY OF CONGRESS CATALOGING IN PUBLICATION DATA

Mitchell, Richard.
    The leaning tower of Babel and other affronts by
the Underground grammarian.

    1. Language and languages—Addresses, essays,
lectures.   2. Language arts—United States—Addresses,
essays, lectures.   3. English language—Usage—Addresses,
essays, lectures.   I. Underground grammarian.   II. Title.
P112.M49   1984   418'.00973   84-7930
ISBN 0-316-57509-7

MV
*Published simultaneously in Canada
by Little, Brown & Company (Canada) Limited*

PRINTED IN THE UNITED STATES OF AMERICA

*With gratitude for Central Control
and the Corresponding Secretary*

Contents

Introduction: Mitchell's Muse
by Thomas H. Middleton

I'VE been lucky enough to have had THE UNDER-GROUND GRAMMARIAN sent to me since early in its history, and I have kept all the issues sequestered in a manila folder in one of the bookshelves in my office. On the sound theory that anything as good as Richard Mitchell's homespun product should be broadcast rather than sequestered, I have on occasion lent my collection to worthy friends, but only after securing the transaction with all their credit cards and all the keys to all their cars.

When I find a new UNDERGROUND GRAMMARIAN in my mailbox, I welcome it as I suppose some people — devoted fans of different drummers — welcome the latest *Field and Stream, Cosmopolitan,* or *Playboy.*

As I recall, THE UNDERGROUND GRAMMARIAN began as a local organ whose purpose was to stamp out the rotten writing and bubbleheaded thinking of some of the staff and students at Glassboro State College in Glassboro, New Jersey. The first few issues in my files seem to deal almost exclusively with the problems of Glassboro. Of course, Glassboro State's problems were a microcosm of the slough that the English language had slid into nationwide; so it was inevitable that these gems would quickly attract notice, first in academic circles, then among all the host who care about language.

The second issue of THE UNDERGROUND GRAMMARIAN

(volume one, number two, February 1977) states its goals: "THE UNDERGROUND GRAMMARIAN does not seek to educate anyone. We intend rather to ridicule, humiliate, and infuriate those who abuse our language not so that they will do better but so that they will stop using language entirely or at least go away. There are callings in which the abuse of English doesn't matter; ours isn't one of them." Clearly, this early edition is addressed to what Mitchell in the title of one of his books has called "The Graves of Academe."

In this same second issue, he announces the inauguration of the Wind-up Toy Award, which "is presented to those who use *advisement* in public. *Input* and *interface* as well as *thrust* will also earn Wind-up Toy Awards. These words might be appropriate in private between consenting adults. The award indicates our recognition of those talents best suited to sellers of wind-up toys in the streets."

I first met Richard Mitchell when he came from the East Coast out here to Los Angeles to appear on the Johnny Carson show. We had had a bit of correspondence, and I'd told him I'd like to meet him if he ever traveled to the West. I planted myself at the bar of his hotel, the Sheraton Universal, and he came in almost immediately. We had a couple of drinks and a very congenial chat, in the course of which I complimented him on his UNDERGROUND GRAMMARIAN essays. I said that each of them was a masterpiece. He instantly denied authorship of them. "It's a muse," he said. "Something out there comes down and guides my hand."

I laughed, but he insisted that it was so. He said that surely I must have written columns that seemed to write themselves. I owned that on rare occasions I had — usually when I was mad as hell about something — and I admitted that I had frequently written letters to the editor and letters of complaint to offending merchants and manufacturers, and that those letters flowed effortlessly from a hand that almost seemed not my own.

"Exactly," he said.

So there you are. THE UNDERGROUND GRAMMARIAN will have great appeal for anyone who simply loves good writing, for the writing in these articles is superb. Moreover, these pieces, articulate, intelligent, often wildly funny, and frequently dazzling, spring from a splendid mind, tuned to just the right pitch, and fired with an angry passion under the supernatural control of Mitchell's muse.

THE LEANING TOWER
OF BABEL and Other Affronts
by the Underground Grammarian

I

On the
Nature of Language

Hopefully, We Could Care Less

The shame of speaking unskilfully were small if the tongue onely thereby were disgrac'd: But as the Image of a King in his Seale ill-represented is not so much a blemish to the waxe, or the Signet that seal'd it, as to the Prince it representeth, so disordered speech is not so much injury to the lips that give it forth, as to the disproportion and incoherence of things in themselves, so negligently expressed. Neither can his Mind be thought to be in Tune, whose words do jarre; nor his reason in frame, whose sentence is preposterous; nor his Elocution clear and perfect, whose utterance breaks itself into fragments and uncertainties. Negligent speech doth not onely discredit the person of the Speaker, but it discrediteth the opinion of his reason and judgement; it discrediteth the force and uniformity of the matter and substance. If it be so then in words, which fly and 'scape censure, and where one good Phrase asks pardon for many incongruities and faults, how then shall he be thought wise whose penning is thin and shallow? How shall you look for wit from him whose leasure and head, assisted with the examination of his eyes, yeeld you no life or sharpnesse in his writing?

READERS often ask about the source of the elegant and old-fashioned sentence that appears somewhere in almost every issue. It is from *Timber, or, Discoveries made upon Men and Matters*, by Ben Jonson (1573?–1637). It was to Jonson, habitué of the Sun, the Dog, and the Triple Tun, that Robert Herrick, another such, addressed his not entirely frivolous prayer: "Candles I'll give to thee, and a new altar; and thou, Saint Ben, shalt be writ in my psalter." The words of the wise are as goads, and we might all grow more thoughtful through declaiming, in solemn ritual, before we put a word on paper: "Neither can his mind be thought to be in Tune . . ."

And if you'd like to be more fussy than we, you can add the part that we leave out: "nor his Elocution clear and perfect, whose utterance breaks itself into fragments and uncertainties."

Many of our readers *are* more fussy than we. They often write, asking why we don't "do something" about people whose utterance breaks itself all too regularly and predictably into fragments and uncertainties. Culprits most frequently indicted are teenagers, television reporters — especially sports reporters, athletes answering silly questions put *by* television sports reporters, government functionaries, and Howard Cosell. There seems to be a pattern there. However, while the abolition of television, athletics, and teenagers would, of course, bring many happy returns, none of them would be linguistic. And we would, in any case, still be left with the government functionaries. And everyone else.

Our fussy readers are mostly too astute to complain about the obvious nonsense of social amenity, although some of them are saddened when instructed to have a nice day, or to hear, from some putative grown-up on the telephone, "Bye-bye." They begin to itch when they hear things like "irregardless," "between you and I," and the much castigated but apparently invincible "hopefully." They are exasperated, at the least, to hear that style of discourse in which not only young people but also many entertainers (including athletes), artsy-craftsy folk, populistical professors, and even some vegetarians, seem forever trapped, the wandering recitation copiously punctuated with "see?" "like," and "y'know."

Hopefully, we could care less about such things, and *hopefully* is exactly *how* we would care less if we *did* care less. We care a little, just enough to preclude hope, but not enough to make us want to "do something."

There is a big difference between talk and writing. They are not merely optional ways of expressing the same substance. Talking is normally a social act; writing, unless it is simply copying the given, must be private. It needs the "leasure and head, assisted with the examination of the eyes," time, solitude, a visible record, and attention.

How we speak, in the press of the moment, is usually the result of habit. How we write, in solitary thoughtfulness, *can* be the result of choice. Our educationists are socializers with political intentions. They fear the choices of the solitary mind, which is why they prefer "teaching materials" to *a* book by *a* person, and they imagine understanding in the collective, which is why they "teach" by rap session and send out questionnaires. If you nag about speech habits that annoy you, those people will gladly offer "literacy" through *other* habits inculcated by *more* courses in speech and interpersonal communication.

The substitution of genteel habits for vulgar habits is not education. It's just a *different* indoctrination. So try to put Howard Cosell like out of your mind, you know?

[V:7, October 1981]

The Leaning Tower of Babel

H ERE at Glassboro State, we have no language requirements. Nor do we have any *foreign* language requirements. This may seem strange to someone out in the
world, but most of us think it a very good and proper thing.
In fact, to suggest the possibility of a language requirement around here is like asking for a bacon sandwich at a
bar mitzvah in Brooklyn.

There are — let's face it — certain subjects that are just
not suitable for study in the schools, and one of them is
foreign language. The study of *any* foreign language is an
egregiously unhumanistic enterprise in which even *good*
students can actually make an indubitable *error!* That's
humiliating and undemocratic. The students who make
many errors will suffer regular and irretrievable diminu-
tions of self-esteem, and those who make only a few will
stand in danger of becoming elitists. Those are risks that
we cannot and *will* not take, especially with all those earnest young people who truly love children and, resisting
the lure of the lucrative but inhumane careers that they
might have found in commerce and technology, have come
to us to be made into *professionals* of schoolteachering.

And fortunately, while we do still *permit* the study of a
few foreign languages here, we find that most of our incip-

ient schoolteachers don't even *need* to be advised to choose Puppetry Workshop or the History of Jazz rather than French or German as what we call "humanities electives." *They* know a humanity when they see one.

There's nothing humane about irregular verbs, and an obsession with foreign language is even more dehumanizing for the teachers than for the students. The teachers are supposed to *know* the irregular verbs. And the case endings — *all* of them. And the use of the imperfect subjunctive. And thousands of un-American idioms. You can be pretty damn sure that any teacher who is actually an *expert* in some foreign language has put more effort into rote learning than into relating to self and others, and will almost certainly be more interested in the mere facts of a narrow discipline of dubious relevance than in the *true* goals of education: appreciation, awareness, global and/or environmental consciousness, and rap sessions on death and Gay Rights. We are not the least bit interested in turning out *that* sort of teacher, thank you.

And furthermore, these people who indulge in foreign language study often pick up some uppity, anti-social notions about *language itself.* They start getting persnickety about what they are pleased to call "accuracy," and they snootily pretend that they can't understand what it means to experientially enhance some aspects of remediation implementation in the sphere of interpersonal communication, which tells you how little they really care about self-expression and creativity, a couple of our *other* true goals.

But there's nothing to worry about. Our Division of *Professional* Studies — an *airborn* division at that — will see to it that there is never a foreign language requirement *here.* Why, just last year, when our little foreign language department proposed a few reading courses that just *might,* some day, be required by a couple of other little departments with no discernible future and thus little to lose, our *professionals*, who make the rules for the curriculum committee, thank goodness, nipped that little old foot in the door right in the little old bud. Those ivory tower foreign language teachers had neglected (heh heh) to list the expected *student outcomes* of foreign language reading courses! You see? The teachers themselves can't find a good excuse for studying foreign languages.

However, while there is no danger of an eruption of foreign language study at Glassboro, trouble looms elsewhere in Academe. We have heard reports of schools, and some of them *public* schools, once again offering courses in *Latin!* And of students actually *taking* them instead of alternative lifestyle education or the poetry of rock and roll. And, even worse, along comes a certain Cynthia Parsons, suggesting (we guess), in the *Christian Science Monitor*, that *teachers* should study foreign languages as part of their training! Can you believe it? How long do you suppose our teacher academy, or any other, could survive such a bizarre requirement? Hell, if our teacher trainees were *that* kind of people, the kind who memorize and fuss about trivial details, they wouldn't make very good teachers, now would they? And many of them probably wouldn't even *have* to become teachers!

We haven't actually *read* Cynthia Parsons' essay, of course, and we're not about to. We've heard it all before. Besides, we *have* read Gerald W. Brown's cogent answer to Parsons, excerpts from which we have reprinted below for your edification.

That Brown is a man with plenty on the sphere. Notice how wisely he eschews any vain discussion of that tired old elitist notion that the study of foreign language has some sort of effect on the habits and discipline of the mind. He sticks to the *facts*. And it is a fact, by golly, that many of those kids suckered into foreign language study *could* find themselves, ten years later, if then, in that entirely different *sphere*. And for the hapless student of *Latin*, it could take even *longer*.

By the same logic — and it's high time that we started paying it more than lip service — we've been wasting a lot of time, time that could be devoted to career education, on stuff like physics and trigonometry. We have, to be sure, seen to it that very few students will actually *take* such courses, but their mere existence is a continuous drain on energies and funds that could better be spent in truly *humanistic* enterprises. How many of our students, after all, will *ever* end up, never mind in ten years, in physics spheres or trigonometry spheres?

And any who *do* can always, as Brown correctly points out in the case of those few who *choose* to learn some foreign language purely for personal profit, learn all the physics or trigonometry they please, along with any *other* narrow specialization that suits them, at one of those *commercial* schools. The commercial schools do not share our high standards. They'll teach *anything,* anything at all, without the least concern for its social utility or its potential for creativity enhancement or even its suitability for mainstreaming. All *they* do is *teach*. They don't even care about behavioral objectives.

And, as only a professor of education could, Brown explodes the old "international understanding" myth by discovering that a knowledge of French will *not* help you with the international *situation* in China. Or even Japan. Professors of education know *all about* international understanding and the *right* way to foster it. They're the ones who *showed* us how to enhance intercultural multi-ethnic appreciation through folk-dances of many lands, and how to teach children to relate to the Eskimo experience by chewing blubber.

Brown makes many fine points, but his last is his best. What is it with you laymen? We've already *shown* you that

A Little Heavy Thinking

from Gerald W. Brown
Professor of Education
California State University

How can we justify eight years of study of a foreign language when the foreign travel of the student may (probably ten years later) be in an entirely different sphere?

How can we justify intensive study of a foreign language when our "track record" in achieving fluency is so poor?

How can we justify the study of foreign language when such a large percentage of our population never meets up with a native speaker? Not only does the student get no practice, but also he acquires no motivation.

Some attention should be given to [the] claim that the failure to study a foreign language is [a] detriment to international understanding. Although such a statement would be difficult to demonstrate one way or the other, it is difficult to see how a knowledge of French would help understanding of the international situation in China, Japan, etc.

In my own sphere the people who are multilingual do not stand out as having a significant international understanding nor as educated men. I admit that monolingualism may be bad for business, and business may very well provide opportunities for their employees to learn, in a commercial language school, the specific language they need at the specific time they need it. Three essentials of language study come together at that point: (1) an able learner, (2) motivation to study, and (3) a ready opportunity to put the study into practice.

As for teaching every student in our schools and colleges a second language, how are we doing with English?

we're not even teaching *English*, and here you are nagging us to teach some ridiculous *foreign* languages! And if, as Brown astutely reminds us, our poor track record in achieving fluency proves that it is pointless to teach a foreign language for eight years, what does our track record in *twelve* years of teaching English prove?

Brown is right. If you want your kids to learn narrow academic specializations, why don't you just send them to commercial schools? *Our* business is *quality* education.

[V:9, December 1981]

The Proud Walkers

When I hear the hypercritical quarreling about grammar and style, the position of the particles, etc., etc., stretching or contracting every speaker to certain rules, . . . I see they forget that the first requisite and rule is that expression shall be vital and natural, as much as the voice of a brute, or an interjection: first of all, mother tongue; and last of all, artificial or father tongue. Essentially, your truest poetical sentence is as free and lawless as a lamb's bleat. The grammarian is often one who can neither cry nor laugh, yet thinks he can express human emotions. So the posture-masters tell you how you shall walk, . . . but so the beautiful walkers are not made.

THOSE are Thoreau's words, and we wish that we had read them years ago, instead of just last week. It has taken us years to reach an understanding that Thoreau could have given us in less than a minute. No matter how hard you try to be thoughtful, ignorance must set you to reinventing the wheel.

We once did fuss a bit over "particles, etc., etc.," but even then we held that the splitting of infinitives, for instance, was, like the celibacy of the clergy, a matter of discipline rather than doctrine. We have not been deaf to the lamb's bleat. "It is often true," we have said, "that the language of the unschooled (so unlike the language of the schoolers) is clear, accurate, powerful, and even beautiful, for those merits do not depend on tricks of grammar." And we have often lacerated the inane or mendacious language of the schoolers who cannot achieve any one of those merits even when they *have* achieved the "basic minimum competency" thought suitable to their kind.

So we are far less chastened than encouraged and enlightened by Thoreau's words. He has given us the key, the *mot* so *juste* that we suddenly remember that *juste* is a word that goes with *justice*. How better can we understand the affected and improbable language of the educationist than as the unwittingly ludicrous display of the smug posture-master?

But Thoreau gives even us more. The proper work of the wise is surprisingly often nothing more than providing the rest of us with exactly the right words. So it is that new ways of understanding come forth, for *understanding* is the making of statements, and statements about statements. In one happy phrase, Thoreau has made the fine and unexpected distinction between Mother Tongue, a concept so familiar that we usually don't stop to think about what we might take it to mean, and the unfamiliar Father Tongue, which has always been lurking in the possibilities of language. Thinking, after all, is nothing more than rummaging about in the possibilities of language. And the thinker is one who regularly answers the question that ordinarily puts an end to thought: What more can I say?

Accordingly, we have gone rummaging through back issues looking for examples through which we might understand that "artificial or father tongue." It was easy. We quickly found these three:

The findings suggest that psychosexuality constructs of agency/communion can be meaningfully operationalized to reflect the degree of psychosexuality integration, with different modes of manifestations and different correlates of interpersonal behavior associated with various levels on the integration continuum.

The multiple issues raised suggests that a particular type of *structure* and *composition* . . . is required. Thus, the accomplishment of the aforementioned aims require that the meeting be from a more *comprehensive perspective.*

Linguistics has become a magic word in language instruction of today. Vigorous activity . . . has stretched linguistics beyond . . . esoteric enclaves . . . and brought it cascading down through the high school and elementary grades.

The first of those passages is the prissy pirouette of the practiced posture-master. Ah, what skills. How prettily he prances from the operationalization of constructs to the reflection of *the* degree of integration, and gracefully glides on into modes of manifestation and correlates associated with levels on the continuum. Ah, how smart he must be. And how *professional.* How proud of him his mother must be, although probably *not,* we'd be willing to wager, nearly as proud of him as he is of himself. The attribute that always leaks out of such writing is that supposed virtue that educationalists have chosen, ignoring logic in the service of sentimentality, as both a requisite to education *and* its best reward — Self-esteem.

The voice of that passage, however, is not just the voice of self-esteem. It is the voice of a *man* full of self-esteem. It is the pompous voice of self-awarded authority, the voice of command, the mighty voice from "above," in which no decent human should speak. It is Father Tongue.

The second passage is an example of failed Father Tongue. Close, but no cigar. The writer is evidently an apprentice posture-master. He does want to strut with the proud walkers, but he keeps on stumbling because he hasn't learned to tie his shoelaces. He is Huxley's snotty little seminarian, who dresses up in the bishop's flashy regalia. His grammatical gaucheries would be inconsequential if his language were "vital and natural," but in the context of that pretentious jargon, they are laughable calamities.

The third writer is just a little boy who thinks it would be *really neat* to grow up to be a posture-master some day. So far, he has neither the words nor the tune, but he is quite as eager to be a proud walker as Tom Sawyer is to be a highwayman, who will hold his victims for "ransom," as it says "in the books," even though he has never felt the need to stop and reckon what that *means*.

Our habitual scrutiny of language has confirmed us in sexism. Men and women are different, essentially and (we hope) ineradicably. Men don't grow up. Pure seriousness seizes only a few of them, and only from time to time. They pretend to be something. They pretend to be sages or soldiers, or anything in between. Even the most witless and inept can find some system, made *by* men and *for* men, that will pay him for pretending to be a superintendent of schools, or a language arts facilitator, or something. And the score is kept in those sad games not by what one gets done, but by how one plays, which means, among other things, doing one's "work" exclusively in Father Tongue.

The crusty Dr. Johnson, in one of his most outrageous wisecracks, opined that listening to a woman preaching a sermon would be like watching a dog walking on its hind legs. We would be astonished *not* that she might do it well, but that she does it *at all*. Tsk, we used to think. That is *not* a nice thing to say. We were wrong. In fact, *nice* is exactly what it is — look it up, if you must — for it makes a fine and subtle distinction.

Johnson knew the difference between Father Tongue and Mother Tongue. He knew what he meant by "preaching," an exercise in the artificial language used by *men* for saying exactly what they are supposed to say. Misogynist though he was, Johnson knew that no woman, uncompelled, would ever *do* such a thing.

Yes, we do know that there are dippy women who *want* to speak Father Tongue, who understand no more than most men how pitiable a display they make of their captivity, for it *is* captivity, not liberation. A man who speaks Mother Tongue can make his own place. A woman who speaks Father Tongue might fill a vacancy in the ranks of the proud walkers. And she'd better have good, strong hind legs.

[VI:5, May 1982]

To be to Some Chewed Books Tasted Are Swallowed to Digested, and Others be, and Some be Few

NEVER spoken truer were words. And out are to quickly some spat be. Unfortunately, however, the natural good sense which instructs even very small children to spew noxious substances clean across the room is suppressed in the schools as anti-social and little conducive to the self-esteem of the teachers. The wretched little tykes, once the iron door of the schoolhouse clangs shut behind them, are required *by law* to swallow everything fed them by the bold, innovative thrusters who make up the ever-changing menu. Peanut butter guacamole yesterday, potato chips in aspic tomorrow, but never a smidgen of jam today.

Nevertheless, however improbable and nauseous their concoctions, it is usually possible to figure out what it is that they either imagine or pretend that they will accomplish. But now, in an unbook called *Expressways*, a sixth-grade "reading" text, we have a disgusting mess of un-identifiable substance whose supposed purpose we cannot even begin to guess.

It pretends to be an exercise in "correcting word or-der," and begins by asserting that "word order affects the meaning of a sentence," as some precocious (and thus, as you will see, disruptive) children will have noticed even before they reached the sixth grade. The exercise asks the students to do something about some supposedly garbled sentences. Some of them actually *are* garbled:

magician a Merlin was

Arthur enchanted an stone of pulled out sword of

Not quite as much fun as a barrel of monkeys, perhaps, but close. Even the dullest students should be able, as

Behavior Modification

in the Classroom Situation

instructed, to "rewrite each group of words to make a clear and sensible sentence." But *why*, dammit? *Why?*

Is this what those educationists mean by "problem-solving"? Do they imagine, or pretend, that a garbled sentence is a "problem" for which all readers must be prepared lest they fail to comprehend deliberate distortions?

Is it some "life-skill" enhancement intended to insure that the students will still be able to check the right boxes on comprehension tests when all the printers have gone mad? Are students, in fact, likely to *write* such garbled sentences?

To make a bad thing worse, the concocters of this silliness can't even *garble* skillfully. Having vouchsafed that "word order affects the meaning of a sentence," and having asked that students assemble "clear and sensible sentences" from "groups of words" that could never occur naturally, these reading experts proceed to dream up "problems" of this kind:

> *the knights made out of marble sat at a round table*
>
> *persons in distress rescued the knights*
>
> *some knights went in search of holy objects on quests*

Try now to imagine the plight of those unlucky sixth graders — there are plenty of them — who can see, as anyone but a reading expert might, that those "groups of words" *are* "clear and sensible." If there is anything at all "wrong" about them, it is only that they will not win approval from the teacher, who can easily discover, by looking it up in the handy teacher's guide that comes with *Expressways*, that *those* clear and sensible sentences are not *the* clear and sensible sentences that the reading experts had in mind, not the "correct" solutions to "problems" that would never have existed in the first place if it weren't for the fact that the reading experts always need tricky new gimmicks to put in their unbooks.

The exercise pretends to ask a question about grammar, the system of principles by which we all, sixth-grade children included, can and do form any of an infinite number of possible sentences, including the three supposed "problems" cited above. But in fact, it asks a question to be answered out of that minimal kind of reading that is really nothing more than the reception of communication.

And, probably for the remediation of those obstinate students who persist in suspecting that it is by form, not content, that a sentence is a sentence, there is a postscript to all this absurdity. It's called "Interaction":

> *Make up your own scrambled sentences about how Merlin could help you. Have a classmate unscramble your sentences.*

It's not enough, you see, although it *is* required, that educationists commit nonsense. They are, as they are always saying, such giving and sharing people. And when *they* commit nonsense, *everyone* commits nonsense.

[VI:8, November 1982]

Lazy over brown the jumped dog fox the quick?

II

Reading
and Writing a la Mode

Professional primates project proposed!

Chimps outshine chumps, TUG study reveals!

On the left: The annual cost of the average HEW evaluator, not including travel. On the right: The cost of 25 chimpanzees doing the same work, bananas and diapers included, as well as travel expenses based on prevailing United Parcel Service rates.

Yes, Virginia, there is a Free Lunch

THANKS to U.S. Representative Robert W. Daniel, of Virginia, we now have the complete text of an infamous document that newspapers around the country treated briefly and facetiously last summer. It is an evaluation of a remedial math and writing program in the public schools of Hopewell, Virginia. The author, whose name appears nowhere on the document, is a functionary — how right that ugly word seems just now — of HEW. The function of this tax-supported functionary was to judge whether or not the remedial program merited continued tax support of its own. Here are some of his (her?) comments. In each case, what you see is the functionary's complete response to a question on the evaluation form:

The objectives were not to specified are the measureable participants that involves to the fullest extent practicable to the total educational resources

_____

evidence demonstrated by the standardized achievement test data was surfaced to the desegregation elimination, reduction, and prevention of minority group isolation.

_____

there is no realistically promises that addresses the needs identified in the proposes program.

_____

sufficient magnitude in relation to the number of participants cost of project components, contains evidence of the proposes project & a very measureable amount of funds are very specified in the project program.

Let's take what comfort we can from this gibberish. We have learned that there is, in fact, a tax-supported program in which the amount of funds actually *are* very specified and even "measureable." It had always seemed otherwise. Nevertheless, in spite of that cheery news, there's still one little cloud, no larger than a consultant's outstretched paw, on the educational horizon. Even as we sit here, innocently enjoying the thought that there is, just as we had suspected all along, no realistically promises, some people are at work planning to hire more such evaluators in a cabinet-level Department of Education. If those education people can achieve stuff like that as a mere satrapy of HEW, imagine what they'll be able to do when the training wheels come off.

It was not out of wisdom, but weariness, that our Congress failed in its latest session to visit upon us a Department of Education. After all, bureaucrats and educationists* deserve a full-employment act too, and a DOE will provide featherbeds for whole new bands of them. They will, in turn, hire herds of the linguistically handicapped to evaluate all the remedial programs for the linguistically handicapped in places like Hopewell, Virginia. So there

---

*For "professional" educationists, teachers are the grunts, administrators, the officers. Any variety of "doctorate" in education, therefore, is a way to get out of the trenches and become a vice-principal or a counsellor, an assistant director or a coordinator, a supervisor or an advisor, anything, anything but a teacher. More than 60 percent of those who manage to eke out doctorates in education, typically through tabulating the answers to an inane questionnaire, do in fact escape the classroom. (*Digest of Education Statistics: 1977–78*, p. 121.) Once bedded down, these folk cheerfully provide each other with meetings to attend, reports to generate, guidelines to follow, goals to implement, instruments to devise, and findings to seek. A Department of Education makes a splendid trough for their trotters.

is, indeed, no realistically promises, but there sure as hell is a free lunch.

Well, we don't begrudge them comfortable berths in Washington. At least they're not on welfare, and most of them are securely institutionalized out of the sight of impressionable children. All we ask of them, when they come into their kingdom, is that they toss us one tiny crumb, advancing thereby the cause of pedagogical theory and even saving us all a few bucks.

Our studies have shown that chimpanzees can actually grasp Bic Bananas and brandish them about, both to and fro. Whenever their Bananas happen to touch flat surfaces, they produce very interesting marks. Chimps, as you surely know, have already mastered sign language and abstract impressionism, both of which would seem beyond the capacities of a typical HEW evaluator. With a little training, chimpanzees could surely be taught to keep their Banana marks on the page, thus producing documents every bit as useful as the one quoted above.

The current evaluators wouldn't have to be displaced. We could save money simply by not hiring any new ones and training those we now have to such a level of competence that they will actually be able to clean more than just one cage each.

[II:8, November 1978]

A Minimum Competence to all, and to all a Good Night!

WE are now ready to explain the minimum competence testing mania that stalks the land and that our
educationists have embraced as a reasonable academic fac-
simile of disco dancing. In this life, the frivolous nitwits
seem to have all the fun. Educationists are not frivolous,
but they are entitled to their fun, too.

Here's how they get it: First, you have to imagine a
herd of people. Let's call them Herd A. They are different from each other in many ways, but, in at least one
way, they're much alike. They are about equally literate.
Here's how most of them write English:

Our school's cross-graded multi-ethnic, individualized learning
program is designed to enhance the concept of an open-ended
learning program with emphasis on a continuum of multi-ethnic,
academically enriched learning using the identified intellec-
tually gifted child as the agent or director of his own learning.
Major emphasis is on cross-graded, multi-ethnic learning with
the main objective being to learn respect for the uniqueness of
a person.

A pitiful case, to be sure, and an urgent argument for a
minimum competence test for *someone*, but it's not that

simple. You must also imagine another herd of people, Herd B, equally diverse but also more or less alike in literacy. Here's how *they* write English:

The time capsule of the 20th century floating threw space finely reaches it's goal one hundred years later. As it is open up information of the past one hundred years is released.

The automobile one of man's greatest achievements for transportation. Now it can not be used because man has wasted all of the nature oil of the earth. It is studied and the result is that man could have develope a less wasteful type of transportation. But the need for power and speed overwhemled there thoughts.

That does have a poignant quality. Finely, indeed, is just how we might have reached our goals, if only our thoughts hadn't been overwhemled. Nevertheless, the passage has some faults. The writers of Herd B also seem less than minimally competent.

Little by little it became obvious even to the dimmest of curriculum coordinators and program supervisors that the public's alarm about minimum competence could be turned into more jobs for their ilk and bigger staffs for just about every department in the educationist bureaucracy. It is an axiom of those jaunty functionaries that there are no problems, only challenges and opportunities, and this was one of the richest opportunities since the invention of guidance counsellors.

So the thing was done. Because members of Herd A are often bigger, it seemed only right that they should test the members of Herd B, rather than *vice versa*. (The testing of Herd A will probably have to wait until the Day of Judgment.) The testing goes like this: That apparatchik who wrote the first passage will eventually assure us that the schools are doing a great job. He'll point to the scores.

The scores will prove that many members of Herd B now *do* understand the colon and can often make decisions about *lay* and *lie*.

So there. Let nothing you dismay.

SPEAKING of *lay* and *lie*, here's a strange item you might have missed, buried, as it was, in the letters column of the *Star-Herald* of Trenton. That paper had printed a guest column by one "Publius," said to be a member of the educational apparatus. Publius commented on the quality of the written English in a summary report cranked out by the people who cooked up the minimum competence testing program for New Jersey. He did not provide quotations, but he did describe some sad mistakes of just the kind we have learned to expect in such documents.

Thereafter, the New Jersey Commissioner of Education, one Burke, set forth his understanding of the matter in a letter to the editor. Like any standard educationist, he suggested that a concern for stuff like punctuation and the agreement of subjects and verbs was "pedantic" and "picayune." So much for education in New Jersey.

Having thus implied that there's nothing much wrong with the summary, Burke, like any standard bureaucrat, hastens to put as much distance as he can between himself and the perpetrators of the almost flawless document. Nobody in *his* department, he says, had anything to do with it. That seems true.

He goes further, however, saying that the summary was done by "laymen" and that the deliberating committees were made up of the same. That is false.

When that crew was first collected, there were complaints that ordinary citizens were but poorly represented. The imbalance was duly corrected, bringing the membership to 108, of which only 83 were "professionals" of education. That still failed to satisfy someone, apparently, for 13 more "professionals" were added a bit later. The final score was: "Professionals," 96; Laymen, 25 (including 5 members of school boards).

At Burke's office, they say that well, maybe "laymen" *wasn't* the best word. What he *meant* was that no one in *his* outfit had done the deed. (*That*, of course, Burke had already said.) In Trenton, "professionals" of education who belong to *other* gangs can be called "laymen." It may be a kind of "cover." Our concern about such misrepresentation will be thought, of course, picayune and pedantic.

Is the commissioner capable of saying what he means? If so, why does he choose to mislead us? If not, shouldn't we be considering a minimum competence test for commissioners? We can clear him of the suspicion of duplicity only through granting his ignorance, and *vice versa*, but it must be the one or the other. Take your choice.

It is interesting that the "mistaken" use of "laymen" causes a misunderstanding so convenient for educationists. As they've tried to blame falling scores on test-makers and rising illiteracy on "problem youngsters," so they would dearly love to conclude that failures of agreement are caused by those laymen.

We have noted before that public dismay about education has been converted into job security for the very people whose failures caused that dismay. Well, that's progress. In ancient times, we used to pay the barbarians to stay *away*.

[II:9, December 1978]

Three Mile Island Syndrome

IF you were lucky enough to have been a reader of this
journal in March of 1978, you may now remember where
you heard it first. In that issue, we (more or less) accu-
rately predicted not only the recent mishap at Three Mile
Island but also the collision of a southbound Metroliner (a
crack train, that) with a hastily abandoned repair vehicle
of some sort. "We are," we told you, "in the hands of
people who say they know what they're doing, but they
don't." We called them "self-styled experts failing in the
work they said they could do and excusing themselves because the work is difficult." Those are precisely the people who smash us into tampers and bring us to the brink
of "super-prompt critical power excursion," as the old AEC
once called "meltdown." It sure is good to know, isn't it,
that there couldn't possibly be any such ninnies scratching
their heads and tapping the dials down in the bunkers and
silos of the North American Air Defense Command.

Curiously enough, in the same piece we cited Adam
Smith's observation that when people of the same calling
consort together, the result is always a conspiracy against
the public. That, in the context of recent calamities, must
bring at once to every mind dark suspicions about the National Council of Teachers of English. In every control

room and laboratory in America, in the cockpits of aeroplanes and the swivel-chairs of agencies, wherever meters are read and decisions made and dials twiddled, this sinister confraternity has planted unwitting agents. Dr. Fu Manchu never had it so good.

It wasn't even hard. All they had to do was convince us that painstaking accuracy in small details was *nyet* humanistic and not worth fussing about in the teaching of reading and writing. They seized and promulgated, for instance, the bizarre notion that guessing at unknown words was more creative than learning the sounds of letters, thus providing us with whole bureaucracies full of nitwits whose writing, at best, is made out of more or less approximate words that might sort of mean something or other. After all, if your teacher applauds your creativity when you read "supper" for "dinner," you're little likely to grow up caring about the difference between parameter and perimeter.

The NCTE worries about the "trivializing" of competence tests by persnickety questions on punctuation and spelling, preferring that student writing skills be judged "holistically" and with no "emphasis on trivia." (*College English*, March 1979, pp. 827–828.) By that, they mean that student writing should be judged subjectively by members of the teacher club (who else could provide a "holistic rating"?), and that skills like spelling and punctuation, objectively measurable by mere civilians, are to be held of little or no account.

One NCTEer, a certain Seymour Yesner, a public school teacher in Minneapolis, questions whether spelling or capitalization "is as important as presenting ideas in logical sequence." Sure. There must be *millions* of kids who haven't been taught too much about the relatively undemanding skills of spelling and punctuation but have nevertheless mastered the rigorous discipline of "presenting ideas in logical sequence."

Another, James Hoetker of Florida State University, laments a competence test "that makes no mention at all of student creative work . . . or appreciation." You can't get away with pretending to teach spelling and punctuation; the facts will find you out. Creativity and appreciation, however . . .

The most pathetic whimper, and probably the most revealing, comes from one Thomas Gage of Humboldt State University in California. He bemoans "thirty-five performance indicators which are clearly utilitarian" and because of which he fears that "little humanistic education can be provided." That's the heart of the matter.

Whether or not NCTEers *can* teach things like spelling and punctuation, who knows? In any case, they obviously don't want to. They want to wear the robes of prophets and priests and peddle to their students the same bogus "humanistic" attitudes that were peddled to them in the teacher academy. They want to preside over rap sessions on values clarification and play charades of holistic creativity and appreciation enhancement.

Children *always* learn something in school, but what they learn is seldom what we had in mind to teach. Children who grow up under the influence of the humanistic education mongers, what do they learn? They learn that hosts of errors will be forgiven for even the pretense of good intentions. They learn that shabby workmanship brings no penalty, especially in the context of anything silly or self-indulgent enough to be put forth as "creative." They learn that the mastery of skills is of little importance, for even the supposed teachers of skills have found comfortable jobs in spite of their indifference to those skills and, not infrequently, in spite of an obvious lack of those skills. They learn to be shoddy workers in any endeavor, comforting themselves, as their teachers did, by fantasies of a holistic excellence unfettered by precision in small details, or "emphasis on trivia."

Then they take jobs with power companies and railroads, where machines and toxic substances, unmindful of "holistic ratings," take heed only — and always, always — of the little things, the valves and switches, the trivia.

[III:5, May 1979]

The Turkeys Crow in Texas

TIME magazine reports that schoolchildren in the USSR, by the end of tenth grade, have been ruthlessly deprived of their right to a language of their own and subjected to ten years of learning grammatical *rules* and as many as *seven* years of some *foreign* language. And there's worse. Those godless communist tykes have had their creativities and self-esteems de*stroy*ed by geometry, algebra, and even *cal*culus, for God's sakes! And not *one lousy* mini-course in baseball fiction or the poetry of rock and *roll!* You talk about elitism? Now *there's* your elitism. Those commies want to make just about *everybody* into some kind of elitist. Why just about the only thing an American kid would recognize in a Russian school is the values clarification and social adjustment stuff. Probably swiped it from us in the first place anyway.

Still, let's hope we don't have to fight with those Russians, an anti-humanistic crew all hung up on mere skills. In fact, if we have to fight, let's see if we can't arrange to fight with the Texans.

Down in Texas, the school folk are mighty proud of the results of their new state-wide competence tests. You might not believe this, but it turns out that *ninety-six percent* of the ninth graders in Texas can *correctly* add and subtract

whole numbers three times in four! (Stick *that* in your sa-
movar, comrade!) And that, friends, means that the teen-
ager in the diner on Route 66 will give you the correct
change ninety-six percent of seventy-five percent of the
time, or *seventy-two* times out of every hundred chili dogs.
And in Russia you can't even *get* a chili dog.

And if you're worried about writing, forget it. Fifty-four
percent of the Lone Star State ninth graders have "mastered" writing. And that beats hell out of the whole *New
Yorker* crowd, of whom more than ninety-nine percent still
have to worry about stuff like whether or not "ambient"
is really the best word.

In the box you will find the topic assigned for the writing competence test and the essays of two ninth graders,
one of whom has *mastered* writing. See if you can figure out
which — and why.

Keep in mind, as you cogitate, that it was not the
schoolteachers of Texas who scored the essays. The scoring was to have been done by the Educational Testing
Service, but the canny Texans decided that they wanted
no part of holisticism. So they gave the scoring contract to
Westinghouse, naturally, and the Westinghousers, naturally, hired some two hundred residents of Iowa City and
a certain Paul Diehl, who is a porseffor of Eglinsh* at
Iowa University. These combined forces, some aiding, some
abetting, gallantly resisted the indecent allure of holistic
scoring and devised instead an austere discipline, "focused primary trait holistic scoring." Naturally.

It is the special virtue of focused primary trait holistic
scoring that it rewards exactly that kind of competence
that we have chosen as the goal of our highest national
aspirations — the *minimum* kind. It takes upon itself, in
the best Christian tradition, the work that God seems to
be shirking. Focused primary trait holistic scoring exalteth

*See page 209.

them of low degree, and, by ferreting out and punishing pretensions to elitism, putteth down the mighty from their seats. That's the American way, and if the Russians would just go and do likewise, we wouldn't have to worry about them anymore.

And thus it comes to pass that, on a scale from 0 to 4, Essay B gets a 2, witness to mastery, and by far the most common score. Essay A, however, is not up to the standards of focused primary trait holistic scoring. It gets a 1.

How so? Simple. Writer B gave *two* reasons for his choice. That is mastery in the "organization of ideas." What is more, his prose style suggests that professors of education and superintendents of schools won't feel too déclassé in his company.

Writer A gave only *one* reason for his choice. However, even had he given fifty reasons, he would not have earned a better score. Focused primary trait holistic scoring is *not* intended for the encouragement of wiseacres like that snotty A kid, and it provides that no score better than a 1 can be awarded to any writer who "challenges the question." You have to nip that funny stuff right in the old bud. You let that once get started and the next thing you know some of those brats will clarify some of *our* values and that will be the end of life adjustment as we know it.

Well, maybe if we make focused primary trait holistic scoring a state secret, some Russian spy will steal it. It's our only hope.

[IV:6, September 1980]

The Topic

Suppose that your school is short of money and can keep only one of the following: driver education, school athletics, art, music, or vocational programs. You and other students have been asked to write to the principal and tell which *one* program you most want to keep. Be sure to give the reasons for the *one* you choose. Remember, you can choose only *one* program.

Essay A

"You have proposed an illogical situation, but I will do my best to give you an answer. I choose driver's education over the other classes on my own special process of elimination. School athletics is out because I can't stand the class and have no wish to inflict it on others. Art and music are really unfair electives to leave out, but they are certainly not as important as driving unless you plan to make a career of them. In that case, I'm sorry but life is hard. Vocational programs were the toughest of all to leave out (and it is the subject your mythical school will probably keep, despite this recommendation), because you *do* make a career of them, but look at it this way: Driving is almost essential to a person's life, and although one could learn to drive elsewhere, it would be much more expensive. Actually, my whole rationale doesn't have to make sense because your question didn't in the first place."

Essay B

"I think you should keep Athletics. Because its good for the Body. And it can Help you if you would like to Become a pro football player."

New Highs, New Lows

Big Bucks for Bantam Books in Booboisie

Slow readers could lead to fast sales, book publishers believe. Bantam Books Inc. launches a series of "high/low" paperbacks, designed to hold high interest for teen-agers with low reading skills. Scholastic Inc. expanded to more than 100 titles a series of paperbacks for teen-agers reading as low as the second-grade level.

The books usually offer simple plots, short sentences and many pictures. Most treat subjects that captivate teen-agers such as disco music and love. Bantam's titles include "Disco Kid" ("All set to boogie and no place to go") and "Rock Fever" ("The rest of his life was a mess, but Doug was alive when he sang").

Rising attention to the low reading levels of many students helps prompt schools and libraries to buy these books, says Thetis Powers Reeves, publisher of High/Low Report, a newsletter.

— The Wall Street Journal, March 20, 1981

SURE, there's one born every minute, but what good is that? That's a lousy 525,600 new suckers a year. Well, shoot, when you consider our infant mortality rates and the obvious fact that a hefty percentage of those kids might escape suckerdom entirely just purely out of dumb luck by being born into the wrong kind of family, the day may come when there won't *be* enough suckers in America to buy all those lottery tickets or support the manufacturers of pornographic T-shirts and keep *CHiPs* and *The Dukes of Hazzard* at the top of the charts.

So let's hear it for those swell folks at Bantam Books, and a big hand, please, for those schools and libraries, bravely bearing through the gloom of back-to-basicsism the glowing lamp of minimum competence and maximum bottom line.

And kudos and laurels, too, for Charles F. Reasoner, professor of elementary education at New York University. Reasoner (what a *splendid* name) is editor and the leading intellectual light at Laurel Leaf Library, Dell's arsenal of high/low books with lots of pictures. As long as America has educators like Reasoner meeting the needs of corporate enterprise, there will never be any shortage of housewives who need to be told that their kitchen cleaner will *also* clean the bathroom, and no one will ever even wonder *why* shiny flakes mean true coffee taste or if deodorants are really necessary, and *Gilligan's Island* will go on forever.

Here's an example of Reasoner's astute editorial judgment, always on guard against anti-social incitements to critical thinking, the nasty skepticism that can actually be caused by so simple a thing as a sequence of complete sentences. It's a passage from *Brainstorm* ("Never give a sucker an even break"), by Walter Dean Myers, also the author of *It Ain't All for Nothing:*

They had not expected the summer storm. In 2076 the science of weather was very exact. The storm had not lasted very long. There was some thunder. A few flashes of lightning. And it was over. Then the strange reports started. People found lying in the streets. They weren't dead. But they had no idea who they were. In the worst cases they couldn't speak.

They were taken to hospitals. They were tested carefully. All proved to be healthy. Healthy but helpless. When they were hungry, they would cry. When they had been fed they would lie still. Sometimes they would make soft noises. Finally they were sent to Brain Study unit for more tests. Then came the discovery. Their minds were gone!

There. That should keep the little buggers healthy but helpless. Give'm a few pages of that every day, and in no time at all they'll be lying still, making soft noises.

[V:5, May 1981]

The Same Old Witchcraft

District Literacy Definition

(From somewhere either in or near Minneapolis.)

The literate person is one who has acquired the skills of reading, writing, mathematics, speaking, listening, problem solving, acquiring and using information, and judgment making. Further, the literate person is one who has developed a feeling of self worth and importance; respect for and appreciation and understanding of other people and cultures; and a desire for learning. The literate person is one who continues to seek knowledge, to increase personal skills and the quality of relationships with others, and to fulfill individual potential.

THE TRUTH, at last, can be told. That Aristotle fellow was, in fact, *not* a literate man. He never developed positive feelings about barbarians. Indeed, the more he came to learn about them, the less he appreciated them.

Franz Kafka wasn't literate either, you know. Like so many other illiterate "writers" — who can count them? — he was never able to develop any positive feelings of self-worth and importance. Hemingway was always shooting off his mouth and never became a good listener. Eliot made some positively anti-democratic judgments, and Mark Twain made some really dumb ones. Even Norman Mailer

41

is said to be utterly illiterate in the quality of his relationships with others.

But don't worry about it. Our schools are doing everything they can to assure that we will be less and less troubled by such pseudo-literates.

The true literates are in the sphere — or is it the arena? — of education. In that sphere, or field, it is almost impossible to find anyone who hasn't developed impregnable feelings of self-worth and importance. So unreservedly do they respect and appreciate other cultures that they never fall into the error of finding anything respectable or appreciatable in their own. The quality of their relationships with others is amazing; they never, never disagree or contend, and they always hail enthusiastically each other's bold innovative thrusts and experiential programs of excellence. And what could be stronger testimony to their fulfillment of individual potential than the fact that they have somehow persuaded the rest of us to *pay* them for all the stuff they do?

Now all of that, as you can discover from the handy District Literacy Definition shown above, is the real heart and guts of true literacy, pure and undefiled. What little it seems not to include — reading and writing and the acquisition of mere information, for example — will simply have to be re-understood in the context of the more important aspects, which may also be perceived as being facets, or else parameters, of district literacy.

Reading and writing are, of course, quite useful. How else, after all, will our children grow up to understand the labels on medicine bottles and write letters of application for jobs and increase personal skills in the solution of Rubik's Cube? Indeed, the promised day of universal mass education through non-print electro-multi-media and relationship-quality encounter sessions may not come as quickly as many of us would like. And even then it will probably be useful if the masses can figure out the wall posters. So we will have to teach some reading and writing into the foreseeable future. However, reading and writing can be overdone, as the examples above must prove. People can sometimes, even in schools, become *addicted* to reading and writing, using them as crutches. Reading addicts especially often become — well, we had better say it right out — they become *critical*. You show us a student who would rather read some book than fulfill individual potential through creative interaction with representatives of other cultures and age groups, and we will show you someone who will always have difficulty with increasing the quality of relationships with others.

You laymen would better appreciate the true meaning of literacy if you could only see hyperkinetic reading behavior for what it really is — yet another of the countless hitherto unidentified learning disabilities. This should be perfectly clear to anyone who takes the trouble to consider what effects hyperkinetic reading behavior must have on *true* literacy as defined above:

⚱ Because he is often exposed, and without appropriate professional guidance, to diverse and conflicting opinions, and the all-too-often cunningly persuasive rhetoric of people who really have nothing more to express than some ideas of their *own*, the hyperkinetic reader often lags behind his classmates in Judgment Making. He is all too apt to say, either to himself, thus exacerbating his disability, or aloud, thus disrupting a whole class and spoiling a perfectly good lesson plan: "Well, maybe, but on the other hand . . ." And just think what *that* can do to the quality of relationships with others!

⚱ The hyperkinetic reader not infrequently abuses the Acquiring and Using of Information in unprogrammed acquisition (and inevitable misuse) of information *not* conducive to the Respect and Appreciation of Other People and Cultures but only to the *Understanding* of the same. That will just not do.

🎗 Hyperkinetic readers almost invariably read works that do not appear on the school district's list of suggested readings, so that they often find themselves perplexed and troubled by materials written at much too high a grade level. Reading, after all, is supposed to be loads of fun. When it becomes a struggle, and especially when it causes negative feelings of doubt and questioning, the hapless reader may fail to develop that Feeling of Self Worth and Importance appropriate to literacy.

🎗 And these people who always have their noses stuck in books usually won't even Listen!

Among the great successes of our schools is the fact that they have always been able to prevent serious and widespread outbreaks of hyperkinetic reading behavior syndrome. This is a remarkable feat, since most young children, even when they first *come* to school, already exhibit morbid curiosity behavior and persistent questioning behavior, dangerous precursors that must be replaced quickly with group interaction skills and self-awareness enhancement. (Children who are properly preoccupied with themselves and with some presumed distinctions between individual whims and collective whims hardly ever fall into hyperkinetic reading behavior syndrome.) Although a few intractable cases can still be found, we realistically expect, and before long, to eradicate this crippling disability and usher in the age of *true* literacy.

Our only problem, as usual, is with the public, where outdated and narrow-minded misconceptions about *true* literacy can still be found. We must *educate* the public. Again. It's time for *every* literacy district to promulgate a District Literacy Definition. That'll teach 'em.

[VI:2, February 1982]

The Teacher of the Year

Daniel Stephenson, of Salt Lake City

As little foundation is there for the report that I am a teacher, and take money; this accusation has no more truth in it than the other. Although, if a man were really able to instruct mankind, to receive money for giving instruction would, in my opinion, be an honor to him.

A TRUE teacher is even harder to describe than to find. We have all known a handful of true teachers, and we can usually see that their differences were probably greater than their similarities.

What was it, then, that made them true? Is there *one* common trait? Are there several? Are there *any?* Can they be acquired?

If we knew the answers, we would print them right here and put an end to the spastic silliness of the teacher academies, but we suspect that nobody knows those answers, that the questions are just *too human* to permit final answers. The true teacher is a bit like an actor or a musician, a queer duck, with indubitable but finally inexplicable powers, powers that no amount of training will provide where something or other that we don't understand is absent.

Nevertheless, we do know a true teacher when we see one, and we see one in Daniel Stephenson of Salt Lake

City. We heard of him because of a fascinating AP story and a few phone calls to Utah:

There is, in Utah, a certain Daryl McCarty. McCarty *was* a functionary of some sort in the state office of a teachers' union. Then, somehow or other, he suddenly became Associate State Superintendent of Schools for Instruction. While being interviewed by a reporter from the *Salt Lake Tribune,* the newly capitalized ASSS for Instruction somehow found reason to mention the fact that he hadn't read more than two or three books all the way through.

We, of course, would have taken something like that for granted, and given it only the briefest mention. Daniel Stephenson, however, is not cynical. In fact, until he came to hear of Daryl McCarty, Educator, he "thought everybody in the whole universe liked to read."

Children, unlike grown-ups, who usually discover in others their own worst faults, usually presume in others their own best virtues. Daniel Stephenson is six years old, and from his point of view, all that unfortunate man needed was a little friendly help. In a letter to the editor, and with a little friendly help from his father, who gave some tips on spelling, the young teacher did his best to bring light into the darkness.

"Make a paper chain," he suggested, little suspecting that it is indeed out of prodigious chains of paper that all McCartys are made. "Add a new loop for every book you read," wrote Daniel, who believes that those who operate the schools actually *have* the values and attitudes that they urge on *him,* and which they announce to the world as witness to the honor of their labors and as claim to money.

"Since you are older," said Daniel, "your mom and dad won't mind. I bet your wife won't mind." And if she *did* mind, he added, McCarty could always "get a flashlight and read under the covers."

When asked what he had learned from all that, McCarty replied, with exemplary exactitude: "I haven't given it much thought.

"Just because one does not sit down and read Little Red Riding Hood, or novel after novel, doesn't mean they aren't educated or can't do their job," says this Associate State Superintendent for Instruction in Utah. "Basically, I don't do an awful lot of reading, it's just not my forte," says this educator. "I don't have a lot of remorse over it." And as to his teacher's best advice, he solemnly explains: "I don't like the idea of taking my flashlight to bed and reading under the covers. It might be suspect for an adult to do that."

Now there's an intriguing idea. Of what, exactly, would he be "suspect" if he *did* read by flashlight under the covers? Intellectual appetite, or some other horrid perversion? Which shall we prize the more: the Associate Superintendent for Instruction who is addicted to reading under the covers, or the one who can do "their job" just as he is, thank you, who smugly tells us that he has "made it a long way without books," and who isn't about to take any advice from one of the children given into his charge?

Daniel Stephenson ended his letter with this: "Since you are a leader of schools, you should try to set the example. You should try to like reading. If you keep trying, you can't help but like it."

A leader of schools.

And that, of course, is exactly what McCarty is — a leader of *schools* and *schooling*, a functionary of a government agency whose purpose is to *do* something *in the minds* of children, through what the Leaders choose to call Instruction, for which they have an Associate Leader, a *specialist*, no doubt, carefully selected by the *other* functionaries for the sake of whatever it may be that *is* his "forte," and that has brought him such a long way.

What can it be, that mysterious forte, which can bring us an Educator of the People as readily as a Ruler of the Queen's Nigh-vee? Can that fine forte be taught? Can McCarty, now that he's in charge, work things out so that Daniel Stephenson can learn it? Can Daniel ever hope to become an Educator of the People by idling away his life with Little Red Riding Hood and novel after novel? Will he go a long way, or will he stay always at the bottom of schooling's massy heap, never an Educator, just a true teacher to his children, never a Leader of anything, just a small lamp of thoughtfulness for those who know him, something just a little "suspect" perhaps, something like a flashlight under the covers?

[VII:1, February 1983]

III

On Language
and the Power of Thought

Instruments of Precision

Their two is not the real two, their four is not the real four.

Prof Prods Pol!

Emerson Elucidated!

W E HAVE long hoped to find a good, concrete example, with numbers, of what Emerson must have had in mind when he said, speaking of those whose minds have been replaced by the orthodox slogans of some faction, that even their numbers are not the real thing. It is a puzzling statement, for Emerson could hardly have meant that they were so bad at computation that they always came up with *wrong* numbers. He could only have meant that even when they said something that the rest of us would take to have a specific meaning, they did not exactly say *that*.

We can find plenty of that, of course, not only in Academe, but even out there in The World, which may be no better a place after all. The big Twos and Fours, which we *hear* as "The People's Democratic Republic of Whatever," or "Quality Education," always turn out to mean *not* what we might have thought. Our obtuseness may require a dose of *Re*education, or, as some apologist for life-adjustment remediation enhancement schooling will name it sooner or later, "People's Democratic Quality Reeducation." *Arbeit macht frei.*

But such examples seemed not quite right. We wanted numbers. Now, thanks to *three* alert readers, all on the mailing list for a newsletter sent out by Daniel Patrick Moynihan, we have them. Some professor (of *what*, you guess) wrote Moynihan, who happens to be a professional politician, some helpful hints for the art of gogy, either peda- or dema-. Here are the excerpts quoted in the newsletter:

> [Your] material had a readability level of 10.8–11.2. This means that it would be considered readable to people who had at least a tenth grade reading level. In order to broaden the "target audience" of your newsletter and to make your message more accessible to more voters, I might suggest that such material be written at a lower level of readability.

Moynihan must be an extraordinarily patient man. Or maybe he's just so busy trying to rustle up "increased funding for quality education" that he can hardly take time off to study the work of the mind as done by the quality educationists who will get to spend the increased funding. Here is Moynihan's reply:

> This is how technique traps us. The intended meaning is that I should write at an eighth grade level, or something such. But the professor has said I should lower the readability level of what I write. Surely that means to make it less readable! It seems to me the professor was not clear.

Why Moynihan calls that stuff an example that shows how we are trapped by technique is hard to fathom. Can he believe that "the professor" is just *too good* at something, in command of *too much* technique, or a master of a skill *too technical* to assure mere accuracy? If so, it would not be surprising. It has long been an article of our folk-lore that too much knowledge or skill, or especially consummate expertise, is a bad thing. It dehumanizes those who achieve it, and makes difficult their commerce with just plain folks, in whom good old common sense has *not* been obliterated by mere book-learning or fancy notions. This popular delusion flourishes now more than ever, for we are all infected with it in the schools, where educationists have elevated it from folklore to Article of Belief. It enhances their self-esteem and lightens their labors by providing theoretical justification for deciding that appreciation, or even simple awareness, is more to be prized than knowledge, and relating (to self and others), more than skill, in which *minimum* competence will be quite enough.

It is possible, of course, that Moynihan shares the delusion, and for all the same reasons. The chosen goals (and probably the inner needs) of politicians are not in any important way different from those of the educationist. But if this politician *really* thinks that that educationist just got "trapped" by his devotion to the stern demands of "technique," then the republic stands in greater peril than we thought. Let's hope that Moynihan was just trying to be polite.

We are not polite. We can say that "the professor" is a boob and a charlatan, and a mealy-mouth too, with his hokey "material," and his just-between-us-realists-no-offense-intended quotation marks on "target audience," and that pussy-footing "I might suggest" when he is in the act of suggesting. That sort of thing is usually just an involuntary verbal twitch, pitiable but disconcerting. (Technique does *not* trap us; ignorance of technique traps us.) But that cliquish use of the word "material" is — well — *material*.

Educationists just don't *feel* right, and feeling is accounted a way of *knowing* in their world, about books. A book is the work of *a* mind, doing its work in the way that *a* mind deems best. That's dangerous. Is the work of some mere *individual* mind likely to serve the aims of collectively accepted compromises, which are known in the schools as "standards"? Any mind that would audaciously put *itself* forth to work *all alone* is surely a bad example for the students, and probably, if not downright anti-social, at least a little off-center, self-indulgent, elitist. Such a mind might easily bore somebody, since only a very few people can possibly feel an interest in highly specialized subjects. And then there's the problem of self-esteem, a frail flower, easily bruised by the unfamiliar, by arcane references, snooty allusions, and, especially, by prose that is simply *not* written at the right grade level. It's just good pedagogy, therefore, to stay away from such stuff, and use instead, if film-strips and rap sessions *must* be supplemented, "texts," selected, or prepared, or adapted, by real *professionals*. Those texts are called "reading material." They are the academic equivalent of the "listening material" that fills waiting-rooms, and the "eating material" that you can buy in thousands of convenient eating resource centers along the roads.

Those marvelous numbers that "the professor" has derived do, in fact, measure something, but not what they pretend to measure. A score of 10.8 means: If this stuff were being considered for a place on our list of approved reading material, we would have to point out that it is only after almost eleven years of our *professional* tutelage that the average student will be able to achieve scores that indicate basic minimum competence in filling in blanks and checking the appropriate squares on a standardized reading material comprehension assessment instrument, which *is* "standardized" because we design it to go with the stuff that *we* use as reading material suitable for students who have had almost eleven years of our tutelage.

If you sniff a whiff of madness in such notions of "measurement," you must have been reading not simply with

comprehension but with understanding. Something important depends on making some clear distinction between the two. Educationists seem to have made, in their practice, a distinction like this: Comprehension is what is shown by the ability to make or recognize more or less accurate rephrasings of what you have just read; Understanding is an inner feeling by virtue of which we can correctly "relate to" people and ideas. Some such distinction must inform their belief that knowledge just isn't enough, and may not even be needed at all, for the accomplishment of the *higher* goals of education, which lie in the realm of attitudes and feelings.

We won't quarrel with that definition of *comprehension*. We will quarrel instead with the educationists' apparent notion that comprehension is *the point* of reading. It is not. Only in some very special cases is comprehension the point of reading — in things like recipes and "reading material." The point of reading is *understanding*, and comprehension is to understanding as getting wet is to swimming. You must do the one before you can hope to do the other, but you don't do the other simply because you do the one.

Comprehension permits us to answer the question: What does it say? Understanding permits us to begin answering an endless series of questions starting with: What can we say *about* it?

The difference can be demonstrated by Emerson's sentence, with which this all began: "Their two is not the real two, their four is not the real four." What score "the professor" would give it, we don't know. But we do know that those "professors" presume that the syllable is the quantum of comprehension, and that short words are by nature easier to comprehend than long words — "sloth," for instance, easier than "laziness." The same applies to sentences; the shorter, the easier. Emerson's sentence is made of fourteen words and probably *is* a bit long for reading material, but it is made of two almost identical sentences joined by a comma, and uses only seven *different* words, each of them a common monosyllable. So its "readability" score ought to be very low. Somewhere in the middle of first grade, any child ought to be able to "comprehend" it. And then?

The professor's reading is not the real reading. His readability — and this misled Moynihan to the *right* conclusion — is not the real readability. It is an essential attribute of "reading material" that it be appropriately comprehendable at a certain grade level, which makes it, at *any* grade level, agonizingly unreadable. That could account for a few other things.

[VI:6, September 1982]

All-Purpose Gobbledygook

HERE'S some swell news from the *Newsletter* of the Minnesota Higher Education Coordinating Commission:

"Minnesota post-secondary education is at the threshold of what may become the most dramatic transition ever experienced in the state's educational enterprise, according to the Higher Education Coordinating Commission. Several partially interrelated circumstances and forces are converging in such a manner as to cause a potentially profound impact on the shape of education beyond high school, according to *Making the Transition*, the Commission's biennial report. Minnesota post-secondary education also is faced with considerable uncertainty, says the report. . . . Some of the uncertainty stems from conflicting and changing societal forces that impinge on education, and some emanates from lack of agreement on what constitutes desirable and undesirable modifications and directions for post-secondary education."

So, did you note the remarkable subtleties of its elegant metaphoric texture? It's *not* the threshold of a transition; it's the threshold of what *may become* a transition. Circumstances and forces, *partially* interrelated (therefore partially *un*interrelated) converge, but not in just any old way.

They converge *in such a manner* as to cause an impact, maybe not a profound one, but *potentially* profound, and an impact that we might well have *missed* had the circumstances and forces converged in *another* way. And that uncertainty! Some of it stems from forces; some of it emanates from lack. And . . . enough. The mind reels.

But here's the beauty part. If you memorize that passage, leaving out all reference to schools in Minnesota, you'll find that you can speak with confident authority on *any* subject just by filling in the blanks! Try it. See?

Holy Cow! Maybe they *are* educators after all. You'll never get experiential skills enhancement like that from reading Emerson!

[III:9, December 1979]

Naming of Parts

LIKE the counterjumper who drinks from his fingerbowl while trying to pass himself off as a peer, the academic arriviste betrays himself by mouthing words he doesn't understand. His sequenced modules and problematical parameters are Academe's versions of bronzed baby shoes and lawn ornaments in the shape of flamingos.

The Snopeses of Academe (who won't even know where to look that up) have problems not only with hard words like *holistic*, which they occasionally spell "wholistic," but even with simple words like *phase* and *factor*. They seem baffled by words that name the various possible kinds of parts.

Their students catch their ignorance. A few months ago, we quoted a "communications" major, a young lady who wanted to experience the segments of the field in order to pinpoint a facet to pursue. She was probably following some gaga creative writing teacher's rule for colorful and varied diction, but she will suffer permanent brain damage if she actually thinks that *segment* and *facet* are synonyms, or that either makes sense in naming the parts of a *field*. Of course, she probably wasn't thinking any such thing; she just wasn't thinking.

And that explains why our educationists and their victims have so much trouble with the naming of parts. You have to do a little thinking — not much, but obviously too much for some people — to understand the difference between a segment and a facet, and a little more to understand why the mind is not clarified by considering either the segments or the facets of a field.

Such thoughtlessness is aggravated by the cloudiness of *field*, which readers of pedaguese will recognize as a handy plug-in replacement for *area, sphere,* and *domain*. Educationists can babble forever about the phases of their fields and the facets of their spheres. There is no need for precise definition where there are no real things to be defined.

There are no boundaries to the happy land of Let's Pretend. If you can imagine that you are *thinking* as you contemplate the facets of your cute little sphere, you are only one baby step away from sucking on their aspects and their parameters. Aspects and parameters are two of the darlingest baubles of the mindless, who find them especially useful in the naming of parts. Segments and phases *are* in fact certain kinds of parts. If you talk about facets of a segment of your area, some rude elitist — from *off* the education field, naturally — may call your bluff, requiring that you describe *exactly* the nature of the parts and of their relationships both to each other and to the whole. You can avoid such embarrassment by hiding in the aspects and parameters, which aren't parts of *any* kind. If you prate about the problematical parameters of the affective aspects of your area, your playmates will give you a D.Ed., and the rude elitists, realizing that you are beyond the reach of reason, will trouble you no more. But, hoping still, they will tiptoe away, leaving you to amuse yourself in your playpen with your favorite words; luckily, they're all sharp instruments.

[IV:2, February 1980]

Forging out, from a very pluralistic Dynamic and Deficits wrapping around a Core, the Criteriology of the Maelstrom of Matrices in the Field at Hand

Also sprach a certain Virgil S. Ward, a professor of education (what else?) at the University of Virginia. We lifted all that neat stuff from a snappy little article called "Washington Policy Seminar," Ward's rhapsodic reflections on a synod of so-called "talented/gifted" educationists.

Ward is not without a tiny gift of his own. He lurches with ease into astonishing figures of speech. He tells of the smoldering welter, the subjugated clarion call, the seed in the scenario, and the maelstrom in the field, in which, most unaccountably, special interests *demand* a place. But such snippets do him less than justice. Here's the real thing:

Thus, in conclusion, let it be said plainly, that in the perception of this observer, for what the thought of any one individual may be worth, our conceptual foundations have deteriorated to the point that action is now occurring in a virtual void of theory. Theory, it can be reasonably noted, is the intelligence of practical action. And science — *i.e.*, that ordered array of the firmest understanding available in any given era or short term period, inviolable logic of inquiry and observation spelled out in the deepest possible constructs of semantic and quantitative symbolization, precluding the elective judgment and behavioral alternative which does not meet the requirements of the most fundamental criteriology which philosophic thought can produce — the particular science of Differential Education for the Gifted is the critical need now still more than in the 1940's and 1950's when its rudiments might have been forged out but were not.

That, alas, *does* do him justice. His blithe blurts of primitive poetastasy are all too rare, like flies in the farina, repellent maybe, but at least worthy of comment. He is more often laying waste his powers by distinguishing a *virtual* void from a mere void and inventing really neat stuff, like fundamental criteriology and the deepest possible constructs of semantic and quantitative symbolizations. That last bit, of course, is the "gifted/talented" way of saying "numbers and words," or, to be precise, the deepest possible numbers and words. And "available in any given era or short term period" is the deepest possible gifted/talented construct of semantic symbolization for the word "available."

If you are thinking that Ward's writing would merit a fat F in freshman composition, you're right, of course, but you've revealed yourself ungifted/untalented. You have fallen into fallacy, not realizing that "articulated developmental experience at the transcendent plane of complexity" cannot waste time on clear writing and thought, which can only be "intra-personal [in*tra*, you got that?] peaks of performance potential." But who better than Ward himself to explain?

Are our alliances in the political process and the preserves of power, such that we can withstand subtle but consequential *mis*-understandings, *e.g.*, that DEG is bent upon the evocation of intra-personal peaks of performance potential among the general school-age population, regardless of comparative status of these peaks. And dare we even raise the question and risk important misunderstanding on our own part, whether the time has come firmly to insist that education in the arts among the general populace, while supportive of the rarer talent, does not comprise the necessary objective of quintessential experience brought into the service of distinctive aptitude and performance potential on the part, now as ever, of the rarer few. [No, he *doesn't* use question marks.]

Ah yes, the *rarer* few, of whom there are even fewer than there are of the merely *rare* few. How lucky they are to have Ward & Co. to disregard the comparative status of their peaks and to provide for them the necessary objectives of quintessential experience in the service of aptitude and potential. The larks will be lucky, too, when the dodos return among us to teach the silly twitterers to fly and sing. Then larks, now merely rare, will soon be a *rarer* few, and we'll all get more sleep, won't we?

[IV:5, May 1980]

Sayings Brief and Dark

In accordance with their textbooks, they are always in motion; but as for dwelling upon an argument or a question, and quietly asking and answering in turn, they can no more do so than they can fly. . . . If you ask any of them a question, he will produce, as from a quiver, sayings brief and dark, and shoot them at you; and if you inquire the reason of what he has said, you will be hit with some other new-fangled word, and you will make no way with any of them. Their great care is, not to allow of any settled principle either in their arguments or in their minds, . . . for they are at war with the stationary, and do what they can to drive it out everywhere.

No, that is *not* an extract from a report of a convention of curriculum facilitators, or a tale told out of school by someone who escaped from a teacher academy with all of his faculties intact. It is — and we always find this sort of thing refreshing — a passage from Plato, who never even heard of educationists, and who never had to. He knew the archetype, the ideal, of which our bold, innovative thrusters are just local and ephemeral appearances — just *our* bad luck.

The speaker is a certain Theodorus, and he is talking not about educationists but about some Ephesians who have adopted the notion that knowledge is perception and, therefore, as mutable and diverse as the world and different for every perceiver. And it is because they deny the possibility of permanent and universally pertinent principle, or of any "truth" that might be supposed to exist whether anyone perceives it or not, that they are said to be "at war with the stationary."

We don't know much philosophy around here, but we sure do know a neat idea when we see one, and *that* is one neat idea. It means, among hosts of other neat things, that we are OK, that we don't *have* to know much philosophy around here. We can perceive just as well as the next monthly. And when you come to think of it, or even when you *don't* come to think of it, you can easily perceive it as a really *democratic* idea, the very idea we need to prove the worth of rap sessions in which eight-year-olds can decide all about abortion and alternative lifestyles and which passenger to throw out of an overloaded lifeboat.*

Theodorus, however, took no harm greater than exasperation from his visit to Ephesus. He was not obliged by

* They actually do this in the schools. It's called the Lifeboat Game, which proves that school has its lighter side. The dull labors of math and grammar are offset by playful interludes of childlike chatter as to who shall live and who shall die.

The game provides a *dramatis personae* clearly differentiated by "socially significant" attributes: age, sex, ethos, calling, and other such contingencies by virtue of which a person is also a local and temporal manifestation. This is *not* one of the contexts in which educationists choose to warble paeans to "the uniqueness and absolute worth of the individual." (Inconsistency troubles them not at all; they are at war with the stationary.) In this case, the verdict must be "relevant," conducive to "the greatest good for the greatest number," and the exclusive focus on accepted notions of "social usefulness" assures that *a* decision *will* be made. Another *kind* of inquiry — whether it is better to *do* or to *suffer* an injustice, for instance, or whether the *common good* is more to be prized than the *good* — would preclude decision and spoil the game, sending all the players back to the tedium of math and grammar. Schoolteachers, in any case, are usually kept ignorant even of the *possibility* of such inquiries, but they *have* been told all about self-worth and how to enhance it.

The children who "play" the game usually decide to dump an old clergyman, a man who is supposed to be prepared for that sort of thing — being fed to sharks by a committee of children, that is. A busty young country-western singer law to spend twelve years among the practitioners of quality philosophy. Nor did he enroll in an Ephesian equivalent of a teacher academy, so that he might experience slogans and incantations relevant to outcomes-based instruction modalities and enhancement facilitation.

We, on the other hand, cannot go home. Athens is fallen, and Ephesians peddle tacky souvenirs among the ruins. There is no dwelling upon argument, but only the rap session, no quietly asking and answering in turn, but only privileged self-expression in the recitation of the latest notions.

We are led into these melancholy reflections by a sad and exasperated letter from a faithful reader. He *is* in the school business, but is obviously still a thoughtful person.

He was filling out yet another of those countless and mind-numbing forms that educationists, given sufficient funding, of course, dearly love to cook up and send around. (They call that "research," and the "answers" — usually nothing more than choices checked off by bored and angry people justifiably thirsty for revenge — they call "data.") The poor man, who is not an educationist, but a teacher, the lowest rank there is in the school business, read these words of wisdom from his betters:

As the individual staff member considers a program of self-improvement, attention should be given to the ability to impart knowledge.

Something must have snapped in his mind. We'll never know exactly what caused it. Maybe it was that lofty Passive Imperative: "Attention Should Be Given." Maybe it

---

will be preserved. She has many long years ahead of her in which to maximize her potential and serve the greatest good by entertaining the greatest number. And *she* is supposed to be prepared for *that* sort of thing — being elevated to wealth and power by a *very large* committee of children.

What a pity that Himmler and Goebbels and all that crowd are dead. They'd make really neat resource persons for the Lifeboat Game. Well, there's still Rudy Hess, and we might even find Mengele.

was the realization that he, a mere *individual* staff member, couldn't even *identify* those of his colleagues who might be of the *other* kind. In any case, he did what you are *never* supposed to do in the school business. He looked at one of those sayings, brief and dark, and actually *thought* about it. Should that sort of anti-social behavior become common in our schools, there would be an end to education-ism, which depends absolutely, like any other cult, upon the credulousness of its adherents, and which, like any other cult, fosters credulousness by giving catechism the name of "education."

The brief, dark saying that caught our correspondent's mind was that pious and oft-intoned mantra: "The Ability to Impart Knowledge." How he thought about that, we can't tell you *in detail*, but *in principle* we *can* tell you, because the principles are stationary. He dwelt upon the question; he did not appreciate it or interact with it. He asked and answered in turn; he did not rap. He inquired the *reason* of what was said; he did not relate to the reasons for saying it.

He put questions like these: Does knowledge *need* imparting, whatever that is, or would *telling* be enough? When knowledge is told by stones and stars, who is the teacher, and in what statements can we describe the knowable properties of his "abilities"? If the imparting of knowledge is the telling of what is so, who can *lack* that ability, except the insane, the imbecilic, the comatose, the irretrievably deluded, or the pathologically mendacious? If, however, that imparting of knowledge is something *other* than the telling of what is so, what, exactly, are its properties? Can we consider the "ability" to do it, or judge whether it *ought* to be done, without knowledge of its nature? Is knowledge not that which needs *beholding* rather than assertion, and is the habit of diligent inquiry not the parent of beholding? As to the worth of teachers, and especially teachers of teachers, ought we not to judge of their habits and ways of inquiry instead of their self-proclaimed and utterly unintelligible "ability to impart knowledge"?

Still, as at least one man we know will surely testify, you *can* learn a thing or two — well, not *from*, exactly, but *because of* those people. Maybe that's the secret of a *good* teacher academy, a place where the students, sitting still and thinking, could just *observe* the educationists leaping from tree to tree in their natural habitat.

[VI:8, November 1982]

The Master of Those Who Know

*And raising my eyes a little I saw on high
Aristotle, the master of those who know,
ringed by the great souls of philosophy.*

knowledge: Knowledge is defined as the remembering of previously learned material. This may involve the recall of a wide range of material, from specific facts to complete theories, but all that is required is the bringing to mind of the appropriate information. Knowledge represents the lowest level of learning outcomes in the cognitive domain.

THAT intriguing definition comes from a "Pilot Curriculum" plan of "Program Gifted and Talented" in the Lakota Local School District. We don't know where that is — the document came from a careful informant — but it doesn't make any difference. Lakota is everywhere.

The definition is miniature rehash of a section of *Taxonomy of Educational Objectives*, a book little known and little read, but influential beyond all measuring. It is at once the New Testament of the cult of educationism and a post-post-Hegelian plan to describe the life of the mind in such a way that educationists might suppose themselves "scientific," and thus win at last the respect of Academe, which ordinarily dismisses them as addled appreciators not only of the Emperor's clothing but of each of his frequent *changes* of clothing.

Luckily for the educationists, very few academics bothered their heads about *TEO*. If they had, the aspiring scientists of educationism might have suffered something more than mere disrespect. However, while the academics' ignorance of this work is easy to understand, for the book is less fun to read than the customs regulations for the import of plucked poultry, it is less easy to forgive.

Although the *Taxonomy* seems to have been sort of "written" by a committee, the "credit" is usually given to its editor and principal instigator, a certain Benjamin S. Bloom. Bloom is to educationism what Aristotle is to thought, which is to say, not *exactly* the master of those who know, but at least, by Bloom's own definition, the master of those who remember previously learned material.*

Even a glance here and there into Bloom's *Taxonomy* would at least have prepared us, as long ago as 1956, for the otherwise unaccountable results of American schooling.

You may, for instance, have wondered how it can be that a generation of Americans seems never to have heard of anything, and knows only as much of our history as the television industry finds it profitable to show them. It may have bemused you to hear how many college students in Miami were unable to locate Miami, or the North Atlantic Ocean, for that matter, on a map. It may have been a sad surprise to discover how many Americans could neither

---

*Bloom is still extant. His latest, and probably most startling discovery is that students who study more will often learn more than students who study less. Such a complicated idea is difficult even for the *professionals* to grasp — *and* "remember as previously learned material" — without a master of those who know who can tell them all about the enhancement of learning outcomes through time-on-task augmentation. And it is of such wisdom that Bloom has fashioned the bold, innovative thrust now widely known, and hailed with capitals, as Mastery Learning. The rules for Mastery Learning, however, and not surprisingly, turn out to be not rules for some way of *learning*, but for a way of teaching: First, teach someone something — some "material," maybe. Next, give him a test. If he passes, good; go on to something else. If he flunks, start over. Keep at it. Stunning. What next?

recognize nor approve certain provisions of the Bill of Rights, and how few social studies teachers in Minnesota were able to make any statements of fact about fascism. Such things are *not*, as generosity, or hope, might dispose you to presume, anomalies, rare and freakish failures of a process that ordinarily produces quite different results. They are in the program.

In the pursuit of mere knowledge, "the lowest level of learning outcomes in the cognitive domain," educationists

are selectively vigorous. They do give each other pretty diplomas for the sort of "research" that reveals that seventeen percent of those guidance counsellors in Buffalo who double as volleyball coaches never studied volleyball in teacher school. But where anyone *not* a candidate for an Ed.D. is concerned, they find knowledge less deserving of high honor, and those who would foster it less than perfect in pedagogy. "Because of the simplicity of teaching and evaluating knowledge," says the *Taxonomy*, "it is frequently emphasized all out of proportion to its usefulness or its relevance for the development of the individual [p. 34]."

Well, there. You see? Who can demonstrate that the ability to locate Miami is useful or relevant to the development of the individual? And if the answer is "no one," how shall we answer the obvious *other* question: Who can demonstrate that it isn't? Who can say — who can *know* enough to say — that this or that particle of knowledge is not worth having?

It is not out of *ignorance* that we discover understanding. It is exactly because of what we *already* know that we can know more, that we can discern organizing principles, and make and test hypotheses, and act rationally. But all of that is not the end to which the acquisition of knowledge is intended by Bloom, *et al*.

That end is rather the typically slippery and empty "development of the individual." To decide that some degree of "emphasis on knowledge" is "all out of proportion" to the "development" of millions of "individuals," or even of one, is several steps beyond effrontery. Some might say that it borders on blasphemy. We are content to call it the *hubris* of invincible ignorance, which quite naturally and appropriately afflicts those who denigrate knowledge. What do *they* know, who know the "correct" nature of the development of the individual? Is a general and pervasive ignorance the result of some "emphasis on knowledge" small enough to be *in* proportion to that development?

If there is an "emphasis on knowledge all out of proportion," to *what* is it out of proportion? How much time and effort should be reserved for a duly proportionate "emphasis" on whatever it is that is *not* knowledge?

There is a word for that which is not knowledge. It is ignorance. But Bloom and his friends must be either consummately cagey or colossally obtuse in championing ignorance.

They begin by claiming, maybe, that knowledge isn't *really* knowledge in any case:

It is assumed that as the number of things known by an individual increases, his acquaintance with the world in which he lives increases. But, as has been pointed out before, we recognize the point of view that truth and knowledge are only relative and that there are no hard and fast truths which exist for all times and all places [p. 32].

Well, *we* recognize that point of view too. It was a hot item toward the end of sophomore year, when its titillating

paradoxicality brought on neat bull sessions as to whether that statement could *itself* be permanently true. However, while the Bloomists seem to admit only to *recognizing* the sophomore's delight, that is due not to cautious thoughtfulness, but only to imprecision of language. In fact, they subscribe to it, and derive from it a grand scheme of "education" depending on the belief that nothing can be known.

It is to support that belief that they must define knowledge only in a trivial sense. As though to prove the vanity of all learning, they point out that "punctuation is solely [that probably means "only"] a matter of convention." We *know* that. And we can *know* its requirements and principles. The *Taxonomy* gladly informs us that "how we pictured the atom" has changed, which is as enlightening as the fact that Aristotle could not have located Miami either. And, most important, because this kind of assertion will lead to the *Taxonomy*'s true agenda, the promotion of "education" as "modification in the affective domain," the demonstration of "what is knowable" concludes by calling to witness "the cultural aspect" of knowledge.

"What is known to one group is not necessarily known to another group, class, or culture," Bloom tells us. As to whether that is a statement about "the knowable," there is a test. Just read it again, putting *knowable* where *known* appears. It is to be hoped that not even Bloomists would say that there could be some knowledge accessible to Arabs but not to Jews, but that *is* what they say when they contrive a definition of knowledge that will permit the inclusion of attitudes, beliefs, and feelings, or any other variety of *supposed* knowledge. Those things, *all* of them "previously learned material" all too easily remembered, make up that *other* category, to which an "emphasis on knowledge" is "all out of proportion" for "the development of the individual." Those are the things that the Bloomists wanted "education" to be all about. And it is.

Aristotle was partly right. Some, by nature, *do* desire to know; some remember previously learned material.

[VII:1, February 1983]

Prometheus Rebound

Of human kind,
My great offense in aiding them, in teaching
The babe to speak, and rousing torpid mind
To take the grasp of itself — of this I'll talk;
Meaning to mortal men no blame, but only
The true recital of my own deserts.
For, soothly, having eyes to see they saw not,
And hearing heard not; but like dreamy phantoms,
A random life they led from year to year,
All blindly floundering on.
> — Æschylus, *Prometheus Bound*

The understanding, like the eye, whilst it makes us to see and perceive all things, takes no notice of itself; and it requires art and pains to set it at a distance and make it its own subject.
> — John Locke

WE CAN now begin to make out, monstrously looming in the near distance, the swelling hulk of the next bold, innovative thrust, the great lurch forward into Thinking. It will bring us, at first, Basic Minimum Thinking. Next, so that consultants and departments of educationism may thrive even in an Age of Thought, there will come inservice thinking workshops, so that schoolteachers can acquire enhanced appreciations of this newest pedagogical modality. Then, either to pass the buck or spread the wealth, there will arise among us comprehensive programs of Thinking across the Curriculum, engendered by the exciting discovery that even in family living courses and driver training at least some rudimentary form of thinking might be justifiable. And, at the end of it all, professors of geography and medieval literature will be hanging on to their jobs by teaching two or three sections of Remedial Thinking.

Although the seeds of this movement can hardly be said to have been sown, they did at least fall among the thistles as long ago as 1981. In the fall of that year, when the young victims of the Basic Minimum Competence Frenzy came back to school for more of the same, the National Assessment of Educational Progress discovered that seventeen-year-olds had suffered "sharp declines in inferential comprehension." The results of its standard test, said the NAEP, seemed to "signal some erosion in older teenagers' thinking and evaluative skills."

At first, before the educationists realized that they were hearing the distant rumble not of a new storm of abuse but of an onrushing bandwagon, they tried to explain away this *new* erosion by reminding us that we had burdened them with the old one. Here we are, fighting for functional literacy, they said, and bringing the blessings of minimum competence into the land! How can we, saddled with your petulant demands for mere *basics,* also be held responsible for the teaching of "higher-order" skills? We can hardly be expected to teach reading, writing, and ciphering, and also *thinking* at the very same time, you know, and without even a penny of thinking-funding either!

It must have been that last point that lit their bulbs. Nowadays they say: Well, of course, we *could* teach thinking *too,* if that's what you want, but we would have to have . . . And their shopping list will make such folk as the environmental awareness educationists and consumer educationists look like shy pikers. As "vital" as all such educations surely are, Thinking Education deserves some *big* money.

And then there are serious considerations, which arise not so much from the silly, self-serving behavior of our educationists as from the ideological presumptions that underlie *all* their behavior, all their practices and beliefs. From those who have never even defined *education* except as anything and everything done in schools, who neither own nor seek any firm principles by which to distinguish education from training, or socialization, or persuasion, or even from entertainment, what can we expect as a definition of "thinking"? By what principles, if any, will the idolaters of the Affective Domain distinguish thinking from guessing, or hoping, or remembering, or daydreaming, or, for that matter, from their most prized "mental" acts, appreciating, relating, and self-esteeming?

And what evidence can we find in the results of their practice and the ludicrous curricula of their own academies as to the quality of the educationists' thinking *about* thinking? Are their inane questionnaires and the jargon-laden banalities of their pathetic "scholarship" the "pains and arts" by which they understand the understanding? Is it through awareness enhancement and arranging the desks in a circle that the torpid educationistic mind has come to take the grasp of itself, and to the power of leading others in that enterprise?

We already have a hint as to what "thinking" will become in the schools. The National Council of Teachers of English has recently discovered that "thinking and language are closely linked." (*New York Times*, Education Survey supplement, January 9, 1983.) Although that may seem a tiny step forward for that crowd, we have to see it in the pale and flickering light of their announced beliefs about the language *to* which they now find thinking so "closely" linked. Will the same rules of cultural relativity and political expediency govern their "teaching" of both? Will they concoct some kind of "holistic scoring" by which, without fussing about the "trivial mistakes," to judge of the better and the worse in the practice of logic? Will they discover *other* thinkings, just as "valid" and worthy of "respect" as that kind of thinking that just happens to be the current and socially acceptable habit of the "dominant class"?

The questions are, of course, rhetorical, for the NCTE has already begun to make just such discoveries. "A policy statement by [that] organization," says the *Times*,

suggested that teachers approach thinking skills from three directions — teaching creative thinking to recognize relationships that lead to new ideas, logical thinking to create hypotheses and detect fallacies, and critical thinking to ask questions and make judgments.

And there we have already three "thinkings," which is only the barest of beginnings in that blindly teeming system that has already brought us a swarm of "educations" and even a little pack of "writings." Soon there will be absurdities like Civic Thinking, Driving Thinking, Environmental Thinking, Family Thinking, and probably even Health and Personal Grooming Thinking, for so it is that empires grow and the goodies are passed around in the merry old land of educationism.

But there is much more at issue here than routine feather-edding, so, difficult as it is, we must try not to be face-tious about the NCTE's "policy statement." (At this very instant, in fact, we are trying *not* to imagine how it came to pass that a band of schoolteachers suddenly decided, by golly, that the time had come for an *official policy* on thinking. Yeah. It's as though the Pope were to . . . Enough! We have to stop this *right now*.)

So let's examine their "policy." Do they truly suppose that "creative" thinking need *not* be logical thinking, that "logical" thinking is not *the* thinking by which to "recognize relationships that lead to new ideas," that "critical" thinking is going to detect fallacies without *being* logical thinking? Is the making of judgments achieved in *one* thinking and the creation of hypotheses in another? Do we need yet one *more* thinking, still to be named, by which to make judgment *of* hypotheses, and still *another* by which to form hypotheses about the provenance of weird judgments?

But again, enough. Such a game of words could go on forever, just like the list of "thinkings." It is by means of such games, and out of a remarkably superstitious belief in the reality of anything that can be named, that they have cooked up such things as microteaching and experiential continua, which can be elaborated (and funded) without any consideration at all of what is meant by "teaching" or by "experience."

In educationists, there dwells the demon Kakepistemé, who spake by the prophets of socialization through Ed. Psych. 101. He diligently compels them to define backwards, and without regard to the nature of what is being defined. As to education, for instance, they begin by guessing that some socially acceptable "outcomes" must be the result of education — making a living, for example, or appreciating a line from *Hamlet,* or being able to balance a checkbook and write a letter of application. Thus, by the educationists' definition, it is *the same thing* that brings about, in one case, the mind of John Stuart Mill, and, in another, the practice of brushing between meals.

So, too, will it be with thinking, for the educationists have no principle to distinguish it from their precious idol, problem-solving. Thus they can say, and believe, this sort of thing:

Thinking is the one skill that makes street-smart kids so adaptable. They know how to solve the problems of the street, and now they have to learn how to apply those skills in the classroom.

Those are the words, as quoted by the *Times,* of one Charlotte Frank, executive director of the Department of

Curriculum and Instruction in the public schools of New York City. If there be justice in the fabric of the universe — a consideration that calls *not* for problem-solving but for thinking — Frank will be demoted to the lowliest rank in education, teacher, so that those adaptable street-smart kids can go and apply their skills in *her* classroom.

So, it is *thoughtfulness* is it, by virtue of which those street-smart kids are what they are? And it must be out of an even greater thoughtfulness — the "creative" kind, maybe? — that their older counterparts, and mentors, are what *they* are. And what of the rats, the astonishing, problem-solving rats of New York, not only surviving but actually prevailing in an implacably hostile and enormously complicated environment?

To lead, however successfully, in the streets or in the boardrooms, a life of problem-solving is to lead "a random life from year to year," a life directed not from within by principle, but from without by accident. There is surely no recommendation in the fact that countless millions lead such lives; there is rather a reminder that thinking is not a "survival skill." While the thoughtful may prosper by thoughtfulness, they also may not. Utterly unlike the street-smart kids, who know just what they want and exactly how to get it, the thoughtful are at least occasionally handicapped in the Great Struggle for Survival by nagging questions as to whether they *should* want what they want and whether the getting would be worthy. If Charlotte Frank is right, if success in the schools' version of Thinking Education comes easiest to the street-smart, then we know something about the schools. We don't *need* to damn the whole system and all of its deeds. Its Charlotte Franks will do that for us, as they always have.

Maybe she just wasn't thinking when she said that.

And that leads to the big question: Who are *they* to teach our children how to think? For years we have examined the dreadful language of educationism, not simply to display its pitiable ineptitude, which is merely entertaining, but to analyze *the work of the mind* as done by those who are charged with the making of theory and policy and the training of teachers for the public schools of America. We have to conclude that the "professionals" who make our schooling what it is must have been standing behind the door when Prometheus was handing out gifts. They persevere in blindly floundering on.

And it's too bad, because it is, in fact, so easy to teach the rudiments and habits of thinking that it could be done *even in our schools!* But first, those who are to *do* the teaching will have to follow Locke, and contrive, through art and pains, to do some thinking *about* thinking. To seek the understanding of understanding, the mind's grasp of itself, is nothing but the first stirring of thoughtfulness. After that, it gets easier, and even children can do that.

For that, we have the testimony not only of experience and Plato, of whom educationists seem to know nothing, but also of one Matthew Lipman, director of an Institute for the Advancement of Philosophy for Children, at Montclair State College in New Jersey. Here, in a letter to *Basic Education* (April 1983), he says something very important:

I find myself quite uncomfortable with the notion that reason and inquiry skills are "higher-order skills." . . . I find skills like classification, concept formation, inference, assumption-finding, criterion-analysis, analogy analysis, and the furnishing of reasons to be in fact rudimentary.

Much more worthy of being called "higher-order skills" are reading, writing, and computation. The reasoning and inquiry skills are relatively simple and eminently teachable. One might think of them, together with mental acts, as fairly atomic, in contrast with which reading, writing, and computation are enormously complex and molecular.

To begin the teaching of thinking with that understanding would make sense, but educationists, hearing, hear not. When they hear that "thinking" is *not* a "higher-order skill," they'll go right back to the *professional* stuff, writing letters of application for jobs and playing the Lifeboat Game.*

[VII:3, April 1983]

*See page 67.

IV

Basic
Minimum Christianism

Uncomfortable Words

*I say unto you, Every word that a clergyperson shall speak,
he/she shall give account thereof in the Day of Judgment.*

W E don't usually trouble ourselves with the jargon or
gobbledygook of elected officials or captains of industry. If voters and stockholders can find no fault in the
babble of mindlessness and mendacity, they have their reward. For the same reason, we have ignored the trendy
claptrap of pop religiosity, stoically denying ourselves even
the easy pickings to be found in what William Buckley has
so perfectly named "The Rolling Stones Version of the
Book of Common Prayer." But even our saintly forbear-
ance has its limits, and Edward W. Pierce, III, a self-
confessed clergyperson in Akron, has exceeded them.

In a recent issue of a newsletter called *minister*, we found
Edward Pierce's prescriptions for "Using the Pastoral Relations Committee as a Support Structure." Hear what uncomfortable words he saith:

The schematized model that follows is an attempt to visualize a
pastoral/ministerial relations committee that will be a support
structure. This paradigm is in no way meant to be a final or
complete answer to the quest for a viable support mechanism
for clergy. It is a model recommended by the interface of the
study, experience, resources and evaluation of three years' experience in my own ministry.

Now that's exactly the sort of thing that *will* happen to
anyone who lets an interface, especially the interface of

the experience of his experience, recommend a model, a *schematized* one, at that, importantly different, no doubt, from an ordinary, *unschematized* model, which passeth all understanding anyway. To be sure, what actually *does* follow looks more like a simple outline than a model, schematized or not, but we can't be sure. This is our first encounter with a model that is an attempt to visualize a committee, a committee that will be a structure. But then, religion *is* a mysterious business, isn't it? It even allows room for the existence of a paradigm "in no way" meant to be the answer to a quest but well worth putting forth anyway. ("In no way" is probably a more pious version of "not," as in: Thou shalt in no way covet thy neighbor's viable support mechanism, nor his ox. On another hand, however, it may be from a hitherto unsuspected translation of a once famous Pauline admonition: "Let thy Yea be Yea and thy Nay, in no way.")

We are not taken in by Pierce's calling. We know the language of the clouded mind when we see it, and we have to conclude, with dismay but not surprise, that the educationists have infiltrated the seminaries. When he describes his "viable support mechanism," Pierce is also describing, and in standard pedaguese, the typical class in an "education" course:

The type of process with which I have had the best success is the problem-solving variety. In this arrangement, there is a problem poser who defines the issue as succinctly as possible; a facilitator who acts as a clarifier and maintains the process; and problem-solvers who compose the rest of the group, seeking to elaborate and support the issue by suggesting various alternatives and solutions.

It's all there. The type is not only a variety but also an arrangement, a series of pointless distinctions, like those elements, aspects, and facets, without which the teacher trainers might actually discover that they have nothing to say. The problem, however, is also called an issue, as though problems and issues, unlike types and varieties, required *no* distinction. And that makes a problem — or is it an issue? — for those hapless problem-solvers. When they ought to be busy solving the problem, they are set instead to the curiously inappropriate task of *elaborating the issue* (whether succinctly or not we don't know), and to the absolutely incomprehensible task of *supporting* the issue. And then there is that facilitator, who, not content even with that exalted rank, insists on acting *as a clarifier,* thus undermining himself by implying the need of a clarifier who knows how to act *as a facilitator,* lest facilitation be left undone.

And when Pierce gets to his outline, the one he calls a "schematized model," he provides the mind-twisting suggestion that the pastoral relations committee include "between 3 to 5 members." Try to figure that one out. Shortly thereafter, we come to item 4, "Choosing and Implementing Strategy," under which we find, of course, as item 4a: "Input and Inclusion of Spouse." There is *no* 4b. So much for the strategy of pastoral relations, and a little plug for sacerdotal celibacy too.

Well, we don't really care how clergypersons think and write, since we are not required by law to drop money into their collection plates. But we *are* fascinated by the fact that Pierce's prose, both in style *and* content, is an exact replica of the mindless maunderings we get from our educationists, who *do* make off with great bundles of legalized swag. Somehow, though, it all makes sense.

After all, the schools have for decades been gradually transforming themselves into insipid and semi-secular churches, preaching the pale pieties of social adjustment instead of teaching difficult discipline. At the same time, the churches have transformed themselves into insipid and semi-secular schools, teaching the pale pieties of social adjustment instead of preaching difficult doctrine. Both have found more profit in peer-interaction perception than in precepts, and readier rewards in guidance and relating than in stern standards. No more teacher's dirty looks, lest creativity flag, and, lest self-esteem be disenhanced, no more sinners in the hands of an angry God. The principal can say with the pastor, "My brother Esau is a hairy man, but *I* am a smooth man."

And smooth they are, and featureless. We never hear in their words the ring of a human voice, but merely the drone of ritual incantation in something not quite language. They are full of high sentence indeed, deferential,

glad to be of use, politic, cautious, but not meticulous. They are Milton's "blind mouths." Should Socrates appear among them, proposing the examined life, or Jesus, saying "Thou fool! This very night shall thy self-esteem be required of thee," they would be glad to interface and share concerns in a type of problem-solving variety of an arrangement, elaborating and supporting the issue and suggesting various alternatives and solutions.

They, who were to have been the salt of the earth, the zest of life's best endeavors, are become a tepid mess of pottage. Wherewith, indeed, shall they be salted?

[V:3, March 1981]

The Other Ignorant Army

"When the community appeals to higher standards of academics, that always kills spiritual values. All those schools like Yale and Harvard started out as Christian schools, but then they got concerned with quality."

THOSE are the words of the Reverend Mr. Rex Heath, quoted in *Time*, June 8, 1981. Heath directs the life of the mind and the search for knowledge at the Mother Lode Christian School in Tuolumne City, California. He speaks as one who might stoutly profess obedience to at least two thirds of the first and great commandment: Thou shalt love the Lord thy God with all thy heart and all thy soul and all thy mind. Sixty-six and two thirds percent falls short of the perfection commanded elsewhere, of course, but maybe it's a passing grade at the Mother Lode Christian School.

Heath is a member of what calls itself the Moral Majority, a populous club of dedicated television watchers who have so industriously practiced tube-boobery that they can claim to detect important differences between the randy imbecility of *Three's Company* and the mawkish imbecility of *Little House on the Prairie*. Other members of the Moral Majority (or, in memory of that president who brought into Washington the doctrine of salvation by faith, not works, the Peanut MM) are the Secretary of the Interior,* who expects that the Second Coming will take our minds off the high price of fuel, and a certain Robert

*This article was written in 1981; the then incumbent has since been replaced.

Billings, a functionary of the Department of Education. In his manual for promoters of new schools safe from concerns with quality, Billings, whose perceptiveness surpasseth that of the guidance counsellor who can detect a two percent drop in self-esteem way down at the end of the hall, ordains that "No unsaved individual should be on the staff!"

The "Christian" school movement (it may comfort some *other* Christians to see those quotation marks) is a natural, but often bizarrely mistaken, reaction to the dismal failures of the government school systems. (Can that Heath, for example, actually *believe* that the public schools incite godlessness by "appealing to *higher standards* of academics," whatever that weird locution might mean?) To some it obviously seems that such a movement is at least a return to the "basics," including deportment and posture. And it is true that many shoestring academies teach elementary reading, writing, and ciphering far better than the public schools.

If they do, however, it is not because they are Christian, but because they are shoestring. Most of the teachers are amateurs, utterly uncertified. They just don't *know*, poor dears, that before you can presume to teach, you need some courses in how to relate, both to self and others, as individuals and groups; that you must be able to perceive and diagnose each and every child's unique combination of cognitive style and learning disability; and that you must be proficient in utilization of audio-visual devices and implementation of remediation via packets of nifty learning materials. Serenely ignorant of all that, and then some, the earnest ladies of the kitchen table curriculum just go right ahead and *teach*. Some of them can probably even *make* lemonade, right in their own homes, from actual lemons!

So the Christian schools — or *any* small schools that can

exclude from their faculties the graduates, saved or not, of schools of education — can provide in a relatively short time that "basic minimum competence" that, in the public schools, is still the misty and ultramundane El Dorado of our highest aspirations. But what then? Is there a life after basic minimum competence? What will be the *point* of reading and writing, themselves only the barest beginnings of thoughtful literacy, at the Mother Lode Christian School, where the vigilant Heath, supported, you'd better believe, by *exactly* like-minded colleagues, sleepeth not, neither slumbereth, keeping guard against diabolical appeals to higher standards of academics?

No school governed by ideology — any ideology whatsoever — can afford to *educate* its students; it can only indoctrinate and train them. In this respect there is no important difference between the "Christian" schools and the government schools, although the ruling ideology of the former is more completely codified and publicly proclaimed. In the same respect, for that matter, those schools are not unlike those of the Soviet Union, which also claim to have on their side THE TRUTH, although the latter do seem to be the more devoted to excellence *in training.*

Having made such assertions, we are led to wonder what hope there might be of discussing them with Rex Heath, and how such a discussion might go. Would *both* parties be willing simply to admit that such a discussion might at least be instructive, and might, at best, provide new understanding on both sides? Would *both* be willing to do the homework, read and consider the thoughts of many different minds, seek and organize what can be known, separating it scrupulously from what can only be inferred or postulated? Could they so much as agree that knowing, inferring, and postulating, as well as the expectably parlous believing, are in fact *different* from each other? Would *both* be willing and able to discern and reject even their own non sequiturs and false analogies? Could there even be agreement that such a discussion *should* be governed by logical principles?

Lacking such conditions, and the skills and propensities that impose them, there can be no thoughtfulness, no weighing of conflicting assertions, no search for understanding, no inquiry into meaning or worth, and thus, no judgment. There remain only such things as beliefs, whims, fancies, notions, and wishes. And bunk.

Those skills and propensities that impose the conditions in which we can *think* are the substance of education, fortuitous side-effects, sometimes, of training, and absolute impediments to indoctrination. The skills are the skills of language, the power of clear and accurate statement, and of coherent, rational discourse. The propensities are the habits of a mind accustomed both to practicing the work of thought in language and to pondering it as done by others. Among those propensities are the certainty that rational discourse will lead to new understandings, since the possibilities of language have no limits, and, for the same reason, the doubt that any understanding can ever be final and perfect. "For us," said Eliot, himself a Christian resolute to the point of relentlessness, and whose works do not appear very often on lists of approved reading in the "Christian" academies, "there is only the trying. The rest is not our business."

And an "educator's" business — if that word, now routinely usurped by the likes of professors of audio-visual methodology and assistant superintendents for supplies and Rex Heath, can ever be rescued from facetiousness — an educator's business is trying, and leading students into all the ways of trying: testing, refining, probing, weighing, inquiring, essaying, doubting, wondering, searching. A *trainer* is properly excused from such concerns; an *indoctrinator* must anathematize them. Thus it is that the "Christian" academies, out of the very principles on which they are founded, can never *educate* anyone.

In that, of course, they are not worse than the govern-

ment schools. They are only just as bad. What is anathematized in the "Christian" academies is, in the government schools, derided as "uncreative" by the practitioners of self-esteem enhancement; scorned as "authoritarian" by the rap-sessionists of values clarification; condemned as "elitist" by the basic minimum competence drudges as well as the smug egalitarians who rejoice that a few of the impoverished children who, if lucky, will spend their lives in dull and brutish labor, can nevertheless balance their checkbooks; and, by most others, whose training in the teacher academy never suggested the possibility of thinking about thinking, simply neglected.

It's no wonder that the Peanut MM thought it good to rise up and smite those troublers of the land hip and thigh. But it's no comfort either. We are not watching a struggle between the Children of Light and the Children of Darkness, but the benighted clash of ignorant armies, in which we, and millions of children who might have grown up to be thoughtful and productive citizens, are caught in the open between the lines.

However, here at THE UNDERGROUND GRAMMARIAN, we're not going to let ourselves be slain as noncombatants. For all that we've been saying for so long about the government schools, and without the slightest intention of re-fraining in the future, we're going to take their side. And we urge our readers (or at least those who are not at this very moment writing in to cancel their subscriptions) to do likewise and not to remain silent.

For us, the decision was not difficult. We asked some questions: Of the parties to this conflict, which is the more likely to forbid its students certain books and to make it harder for *anyone* to find them? Which would, if it could, close down pestiferous publications like this one? Which one, when sufficiently pressed, and we do intend to press, will eventually accuse its enemies of warring against God?

Furthermore, the government schools have one su-preme, if unintended, virtue. They are such chaotic and Byzantine bureaucracies, ruled over by herds of inept and dull-witted functionaries, that some good teachers, genu-

inely devoted to the life of the mind, can often go unde-tected for years. For some few students, those dissidents make all the difference. But in the "Christian" acade-mies, much smaller and tightly controlled, the dissidents are all too likely to be sniffed out quickly by the Unsaved Individuals Committee.

The issue is not curriculum or methodology or family life or even the private enterprise system. The issue is freedom. The mind simply cannot be free without the power of thoughtful inquiry. If the mind is not free to gather knowledge, to form understanding, to judge of worth, and then, out of the best that it can do in knowing, understanding, and judging, *will* what it deems good, then there can be no such thing as morality, a system intended to judge the worth of individual *choices*. The "Moral Majority" must be, in fact, some *other* kind of organization. Its avowed dedication to ignorance and thoughtlessness — Heath is not alone — belies its very name.

Lacking the informed, willing assent of thoughtfulness, obedience to even some presumably unexceptionable precept is just another passion, tepid though it well may be. And who can be led by unexamined precept into one passion can as easily be led into another. And still another. He can be neither free nor moral, only impassioned. Should there be enough of his kind noisily applauding themselves for the "sincerity" and "correctness" of their shared passions, they will show us what Yeats meant by the "worst," who are "filled with passionate intensity."

And what of the "best"? Are they out there? Is there a Mental Minority? Was Yeats right about them too? Have they "lost all conviction"?

It must be so. There is mostly silence, a silence that seemed at first disdainful, then tactful, then wary, and that by now has turned simple cowardice. Those educationists, who have so long trumpeted their love of excellence, have fled as usual into the mighty fortress of Low Profile Poltroonery. Maybe this storm, too, will blow over, or maybe a savior will come, bearing some really neat innovations.

Prudent publishers, busily gathering into barns and ever mindful of textbook adoptions in Texas, are eager to be oh so open-minded. Albert Shanker, hoping the ninety and nine can fend for themselves while he takes care not to lose a dues-paying one, tuts a tiny tut from time to time.

"Know ye not," wrote Saint Paul, who may have momentarily forgotten about the laborers who came late to the vineyard, "that they which run a race run all, but one receiveth the prize?" History, as H. G. Wells said, and that was way back *then*, "becomes more and more a race between education and catastrophe." And by "education" he didn't mean basic minimum competence or an indoctrination impervious to thoughtfulness. However, by "catastrophe" he meant catastrophe.

Just now, there seems to be only one runner on the track, and, unhampered by concerns with quality, undeterred by appeals to higher standards of academics, he isn't even looking over his shoulder.

[V:6, September 1981]

Tongues of Ice

Now when this was noised abroad, the multitude came together, and were confounded, because that every man heard them speak in his own language. And they were all amazed and marvelled . . .

JOACHIM of Floris turns out to have been right after all, except for what is probably nothing more than a trivial error in orthography. The Age of the Father gave way to the Age of the Son, which has by now succumbed entirely before the prancing parameters of the Age of the Wholly Gauche. And that creepy sound you hear, that whooping whoosh as of a rushing mighty windbag, signals the escaping gases of the new dispensation. Where once a few spoke a language that everyone could understand, whole multitudes now recite a lingo that no one can understand.

The Conference of Major Superiors of Men is made up of the abbots and provincials of various Roman Catholic religious orders. On February 10, 1981, a day that they might have spent in prayer, the members of its national board met in Milwaukee for an "evaluation of CMSM structures based on the self-studies." Sounds familiar? And that's not all. A certain Sr. Mary Littell — how did *she* get into the act? — was "engaged as facilitator for the day." Here's how she did it, as reported to the assembled worthies in August. (Yes, even *there* we have a mole):

To facilitate the process, Sr. Mary utilized the Hoover Grid which begins with the recognition of purpose and values, leading to goals, objectives and finally to implementation. The first and

101

most important step is at the myth level where the renewal of ideals, hopes, dreams and traditions takes place. It is the level of identity and purpose for being.

The advantage of this process is that it puts all the elements of an organization not into a flow chart which is static but into the flow of the organization which is constantly changing and dynamic. In the course of the process the board defined the following elements for evaluation:

The tasks of the board membership and the religious communities through them (the major superiors) is one of (1) animating (through clear identification); (2) facilitating (through acting out the goals and objectives); and (3) impacting (through actions on various levels of CMSM).

So now abideth animating, facilitating, and impacting, these three; but the greatest of these is impacting.

You will probably want to practice these virtues. No problem. To animate, just come up with identifications. Be sure they're *clear*, of course. (See above for clues on clarity.) In no time at all, you'll be animating all over to beat the band and ready to facilitate through acting out goals and objectives. Cinchy. And then — on to impacting! Just remember the one, simple secret of impacting. *Action!* Action on *levels*. *Various* levels.

And if you run into any trouble, don't come to us. Go and consult the nearest Hoover Grid. We don't exactly know what that is, of course, but we're willing to bet the renewal of ideals, hopes, dreams, and traditions at the myth level against a wrinkled old Values Perception/Assessment Inventory/Questionnaire that you can find one at your local teacher-training academy.

We know Educanto when we see it, and this report is full of it. It bristles with "linkage," "resourcing" (with "input" from "resource persons"), "networking," "sharing," "cross-cultural communications," and even offers its own bold, innovative thrust in "ad hocracy," which is defined as "creation of task forces for proper resourcing." So where is the Inquisition, now that we need it?

Even the punctuation is typical of a writer who just can't be bothered with the *meaning* of what he writes. There is a difference between "the Hoover Grid which begins with the recognition of purpose" and "the Hoover Grid, which begins with the recognition of purpose." The first, which is what the writer has given us, implies the horrifying existence of *other* Hoover Grids beginning with *other* recognitions. The same confused inattentiveness causes "the myth level where renewal takes place," to be distinguished from the other myth levels; "a flow chart which is static"; and "the flow of the organization which is constantly changing." In *that* one we don't know whether to be confused about the *flow* or the *organization*. Or both. Or neither.

But if *we* are confused, it is because we are paying attention. This kind of language, devised to give the tone of sophisticated substance to the obvious, the empty, and the banal, is always a dreary and disorderly exercise of robot-like *inattentiveness*. The writer's *mind* has no stake in it; he just wants to get out a report that *sounds* like a report. The report is exactly one of those "vain repetitions" of the heathen; it neither provides clear knowledge nor fosters finer understanding, except, of course, in the very few who will actually pay attention. And what *they* will understand will not be what the writer would have had in mind, if he *had* had anything in mind. Somewhere in the dark labyrinth of doctrinal elaboration, there must be a technical name for this nasty perversion of language and intellect. It's probably something like *Impactio.*

Well, we know in part, and we prophesy in part, and in part we babble, with the tongues neither of men nor of angels, reciting what we have often heard, as blind mouths speak to stopped ears, as no one speaks to no one.

[V:8, November 1981]

Over the Rainbow Way up High

W E are *definitely* not in Kansas anymore. We noticed this weird fact only recently, when an itinerant nostrum peddler was accused of some pretty sharp practice and wound up defending himself before a federal grand jury. He testified that what he had done was strictly A-OK, and that he knew this because he had discussed it all in a face-to-face meeting with Jesus. When asked how he *knew* that it was Jesus, he replied that he had recognized him from his picture.

We can't tell you what happened then, but we can sure tell you what *didn't* happen, because if it *had* the papers would have been full of it for a week. So here's what didn't happen: The jurors did not fall down on the floor gasping and choking with laughter. The lawyers did not rush whooping from the room, holding their pocket handkerchiefs before their streaming eyes. In fact, the only normal human thing that happened there was that some nut said something stupendously funny. But everything *else* was weird.

And only a few weeks later, the same mountebank, still at large, staged a nuptial extravaganza in which a thousand or so of his female followers were more or less married up with a like number of his male ditto. All agog to discover more evidence toward an Over the Rainbow Hypothesis, we tuned it in on the TV. Sure enough. They were all Munchkins.

Then along came Phyllis Schlafly. She has not yet admitted to being Glinda the Good, but who else would go floating around the country in such a big bubble? And she does admit that she intends to do a whole lot of Good.

We read about all the Good she plans to bestow on us in a *New York Times* account of a big "Over the Rainbow Celebration" she threw in Washington. (Thirty-five bucks a head, and *no* Tupperware selling!) She took the occasion to announce that she was even going to do Good in the schools, which was kind of a thrill for us, because we do need all the help we can get, even if it comes in a bubble.

Phyllis — gosh, we hope she won't mind if we call her that; it's just that we feel we know her, oh *so* well — Phyllis kicked off a campaign to stock all the schools and libraries with *pro*-family books, presumably to replace the *anti*-family books, by "such writers as Hemingway, Steinbeck, Hawthorne, and Twain," which are being rooted *out* of schools and libraries by her "Eagle Forum" squads. (We don't know what that is; we're guessing that it must be something like the Lullaby League.)

Now we've actually read those writers, and even lots of others "such as" them, but we never have been able to figure which ones, and in which books, and exactly to what degree, are pro-, or anti-, family, or neither, or *both*. Those writers are slippery rascals, who portray lovely families and rotten families, and people who do well, or ill, because of the one, or in spite of the other, or both, or neither, or *vice versa*, if you know what we mean by that. And what's a Mother to do?

So it seemed just peachy that Glinda the Good was willing to take on the hard task of making judgments about books. But then we started to notice something fishy about her powers of judgment.

She said that sex education, which we have ridiculed for reasons that still seem cogent, was "a principal cause of teenage pregnancy." If we had to rely on that line of argument, even educationists would be able to laugh at us.

She said that her "greatest contribution" was "making sure that eighteen-year-old girls won't be drafted," and that she just couldn't imagine "a greater gift." Well, we had no trouble at all imagining not just one but lots of greater gifts for eighteen-year-old girls, starting with the power of reason. But just as we began to suspect that Phyllis might be a bit below her grade level in creative fantasy as an alternative mode of cognition, she proved us wrong. It turned out that she *could* imagine a greater gift, and not just for the girls, but for all of us. "The atomic bomb," she proclaimed, "is a marvelous gift that was given to our country by a wise God."

We can't tell you what happened next, but we *can* tell you what didn't happen next. The party-goers did not fall down on the floor gasping and choking with laughter. Jerry Falwell (a reverend) and Jesse Helms (an honorable) did not rush whooping from the room, holding their pocket handkerchiefs before their streaming eyes. In fact, the only normal human thing that happened there was that some nut said something stupendously funny. But everything *else* was weird.

So it is in the merry old land of Oz: no brains, but lots of diplomas. Honor and reverence, schooled in the "appreciation" of everyone's Right to his opinion, which is as good as anyone else's, have learned to "relate to" Unreason. Logic and fantasy are just alternate modes of cognition, although the one is difficult and so "elitist," while the other is immediately possible for all and "democratic"; the one sets limits and encourages "authoritarianism," while the other knows no boundaries and releases "creativity." Feeling, attitude, belief, awareness, are just as much sources of "knowledge" as disciplined study, but disciplined study is far more likely than the others, which are "humanistic," to bring "mere knowledge" for nothing more than "its own sake." Rationality is cold, a sly and clever stunt performed with tricky language; the babbling gush of sincerity is a warm and welcome way of self-expression, which requires not critical scrutiny, but tolerance for other "values" and "points of view."

We don't see any hope of getting back to Kansas. But if, someday, some teacher tells the students that it's time to learn American history by role-playing the constitutional convention while appreciating fife music, and the students all fall down on the floor gasping and choking with laughter, then we'll be heading for home.

[VI:6, September 1982]

The Gingham Dog and the Calico Cat

FOR some reason, we have not convinced the rapidly multiplying proponents of the back-to-basics-with-the-Bible "education" movement that we are *not* on their side. What's wrong with us that we haven't figured out how to offend those usually truculent and combative enthusiasts? We have had no trouble in offending their mirror-image counterparts, the silly educationists, who hold *exactly the same* thematic belief — that knowledge and reason are not enough, and who "educate" by *exactly the same* method — the modification of behavior through persuasion addressed to the sentiments. The details don't matter where the principle is rotten.

One of those "Christian" school newsletters recently reprinted portions of a piece called "The Answering of Kautski," in which we considered similarities in educationism and bolshevism.* We quoted Lenin's famous line about "teaching" the children and planting a seed that will never be uprooted. We also quoted (and the reprint *did* include) a much less familiar Leninism, saying that most people are not capable of thought, and all they need is to "learn the words."

The readers of the newsletter were presumably confirmed in righteousness by an essay linking what schools do to what Lenin said. It did not occur to them, appar-

*See page 239.

ently, that Luther, to whom Reason was just "the Devil's whore," also said as much, and, in so saying, echoed whole choirs of orthodox theologians.

There is only *one* Education, and it has only *one* goal: the freedom of the mind. Anything that needs an adjective, be it civics education, or socialist education, or Christian education, or whatever-you-like education, is *not* education, and it has some *different* goal. The very existence of modified "educations" is testimony to the fact that their proponents cannot bring about *what they want* in a mind that is free. An "education" that cannot do its work in a free mind, and so must "teach" by homily and precept in the service of *these* feelings and attitudes and beliefs rather than *those*, is pure and unmistakable tyranny. And it is *exactly* the kind of tyranny, "tyranny over the mind of man," to which Thomas Jefferson swore "eternal enmity" on — on what? — on "the altar of God."

Jefferson was not a bolshevik. He wrote to a nephew:

Question with boldness even the existence of God; because, if there be one, he must more approve of the homage of reason than that of blindfolded fear.

No bolshevik can say the equivalent in *his* system of belief: Question boldly even the existence of the dialectical process and the withering away of the state. Jefferson's admonition ought to raise provocative questions for those who like to claim that the Republic was founded on *their* "religious" principles, but it doesn't. Bolsheviks are not the only ones who never think of asking certain questions.

Reason is not the Devil's whore. It is the whore's Devil.

To those who have sold their minds for some comfortable sentiments and comforting beliefs, Reason is The Adversary to be hated and feared, the bringer of doubt and difficult questions, the sly disturber of The Peace. To children who are led into whoredom, it matters not at all *which* sentiments and beliefs they are given in return for the freedom of their minds. Whatever the fee, they cannot judge its worth.

Sometimes it seems that every illusion that cripples the mind is taught in schools. The silly notion that if one ideological faction is wrong the other must be right is planted in our minds by the *belief* that true/false tests have something to do with education. We imagine some real difference between Republicans and Democrats, liberals and conservatives, government educationists and church educationists. They are all alike. Their prosperity depends on our believing that beliefs and sentiments, *theirs*, of course, are somehow *finer, nobler,* more *virtuous* or *humane* than mere Reason.

Half past twelve is coming on, and neither the church cat nor the dog in the manger has slept a wink. Should we do something, or should we hope that they'll eat each other up? Will burglars steal *this* pair away? Will the "Christian" newsletter reprint all this?

[VI:6, September 1982]

V

The Social Scene

I'm All Right, Juanito

If the immigrant who comes here in good faith becomes an American and assimilates himself to us, he shall be treated on an exact equality with everyone else, for it is an outrage to discriminate against any such man because of creed or birthplace or origin.

But this is predicated upon the man's becoming in very fact an American and nothing but an American. If he tries to keep segregated with men of his own origin and separated from the rest of America, then he isn't doing his part as an American.

We have room for but one language here, and that is the English language, for we intend to see that the crucible turns our people out as Americans . . . and not as dwellers in a polyglot boarding house.

— Theodore Roosevelt

There's no one that can set himself up, really, and say you must melt.

— Renaldo Masiez

WHO, you may ask, is Renaldo Masiez? Well, Renaldo Masiez is a functionary at our shiny new Department of Education, where the right hand, merrily stirring up the melting pot with "citizenship education," obviously doesn't know that the left hand is concocting a tangy gazpacho of truculent separatism, of which the flavor may prove uncongenial to the American palate when we receive (and translate) a Unilateral Declaration of Independence from Nueva York.

Masiez himself *has* melted, right into a good job in government, where he's supposed to do something about the Bilingual Education Program. The aim of that program, we were told, was to hasten the melting of some children less fortunate than Masiez by teaching them in their own languages *while* they were learning English so that they wouldn't have to be taught in their own languages anymore. That would not only fit them for life in this country, but it would also spare us the pain of teaching everything in seventy-two languages forever. It seemed a good idea at the time, but only to people who don't know the first damn thing about how public education works, notably a pack of congressmen, or to those who saw in it some payoff for themselves, notably a pack of congressmen. In its ten years so far, the program has cost about a billion dollars and has helped, according to Masiez, "less than one percent of those that were found to be limited English proficient." (His estimate is much too high. We make it approximately 0.0137 percent when you count in all the educationists and functionaries who don't, as Masiez puts it, "receive minimally adequate services" but are obviously, just as much as any schoolchild, proficient in limited English.)

Masiez said those things in a conversation with Jack Perkins on "Prime Time Saturday." Perkins also spoke with the Supremo Director of BE, one J. Gonzalez, who pronounced a newly discovered version of our history. The old way, in which children were taught some English as quickly as possible and put into regular classes where they could learn a lot more, was "very ineffective." When Perkins, flabbergasted, suggested that the evidence did not support such an assertion, and that the Supremo might just be talking through his sombrero, Gonzalez, visibly vexed, muttered, "Well, you could always point to some groups where it has worked."

Yeah. Some groups. Poles, Italians, Armenians, Hungarians, Swedes, Russians, Germans, Basques, Finns, Turks, Chinese, Portuguese, Ukrainians, Japanese, Danes, Bosnia-Herzegovinians, and maybe even a few Bulgarians. There may be more.

Although school work is now taught in seventy-two foreign languages, a great majority of students in bilingual programs are, like most of the people who direct such programs, Hispanic. If it weren't for bilingual education, we could expect that in a few generations those children, their children, and grandchildren, would be living all over this land and doing everything that there is to do, for such was the destiny of "some groups." As it is, we are sentencing them to remain forever in the barrios and to wait on each other in the bodegas. Masiez and Gonzalez, however, will be all right.

The Department of Education has decided that teachers in bilingual programs, once expected to *be* bilingual, don't need to know any English at all. Bye-bye, bi. And children who *have* learned enough English to attend regular classes will be shot right back into the –lingual program should their work ever fall below average. That's a valuable lesson in humility for the students and a guarantee of steady work for all those –lingual teachers.

Imagine now that it was not Gonzalez and Masiez but Ronald Reagan who said that we should *not* require Hispanic children to learn English, and that what may have worked with "some groups" wouldn't work with *them*. Suppose that it was the mayor of Los Angeles who said that the Chicano children should be "prepared for life in the Hispanic community" where they can stay with their own kind and preserve their cultural heritage as much as they like. And try this, from the Grand Dragon of the KKK: "Well shoot, they aint no reason atall fer them folks ta melt. Reckon id be better they don't, an that's a fack."

There can never be equality of opportunity in a land where class is labeled in language. Let's hope that the bilingual boondoggle never *does* find more than one percent of those who "need" it. Gonzalez and Masiez will still be all right (it isn't for *success* that they get paid), and legions of new Americans may escape lives of involuntary servitude.

[IV:7, October 1980]

Voucher, Schmoucher

THERE is very little to be gained and much to be lost in assuring, through education voucher schemes or tuition tax credits, that the public school system will become entirely what it is now only partly — the last, futile hope of the permanently disposessed and disabled. We say this with testy reluctance, and certainly *not*, as regular readers will know, because we can see any hope that the jargon-besotted and uneducated tribes of educationists and teacher-trainers will ever provide the land with literate and thoughtful citizens, but because there is no chance at all that credits or vouchers would destroy or even mitigate the government schools, which have proven again and again that they can easily digest and transform into nourishment any complaint brought against them. As the better and luckier students — and teachers — escape, our cunning educationists will have no trouble persuading the same old agencies and legislatures that they now need even *more* money. But the voucher and credit schemes probably *will* destroy the worth of the private schools.

To see why, we must consider some popular, widely preached misunderstandings:

"The public schools could provide better education if we gave them more money." This is false. We give them far too much money. They spend it on gimmicks and gadgets and programs and proposals and whole legions of apparatchiks and uneducated busybodies and Ladies Bountiful manquées. The private schools just don't have that kind of money. That's why they're often so much better. If we were to enrich the private schools, most of them would hire the recently disemployed values clarification facilitators and start offering courses in environmental awareness enhancement and creative expression of self-as-individual-self through collage. In a few years, we would

have thousands of private schools just as bad as the public schools are now. Furthermore, bad private schools, unlike bad public schools, can do as they damn well please just as long as they can find buyers for what they choose to sell, and they will care no more for our opinions, or yours, than the mongers of obscene T-shirts care about our quaint canons of taste. The people who run the government schools can at least be ridiculed and humiliated in public.

All of that must be seen in the darkness cast by another popular misunderstanding: "Parents should be free to choose for their children whatever kind of education they think best." This is *not* false, for it asserts only a special case of that right to the pursuit of happiness to which we are supposed to be committed. It is, however, irrelevant and (perhaps) unintentionally cynical, for it presumes the possibility of "free choice" in countless millions of innocent citizens who have themselves been "educated" by the life-adjustment slogan-mongers, and who have come to "think" that a good education is an indoctrination in *their* pet notions and beliefs rather than someone else's. Their choices of schools for their children will be no more the fruit of informed and thoughtful discretion than their choices of deodorants and designer jeans. The support they might withdraw, through vouchers or credits, from one pack of fools and charlatans they would fork over to another of the same, which, furthermore, will usually be an ad hoc reconstitution of the first pack, now happily embarked on what is for them just one more obviously profitable, bold, innovative thrust.

We can understand the angry desperation out of which even thoughtful citizens can propose, as remedy for the ills caused by one governmental contraption, yet another governmental contraption. And any system for credits will be exactly that, a wholly owned subsidiary of the state and a bureaucratic agency for the propagation of ideology and the enforcement of "standards." And the standards will be devised not by the enthusiasts of vouchers, who don't really know exactly what they want anyway, but by the same old coalition of educationists and unionists and politicians and social engineers and manufacturers of gimmicks and publishers of pseudo-books, who *do* know exactly what they want, and exactly how to get it.

It is simply naive to imagine that our government, or any government anywhere, will construe tax credits or vouchers as a way of letting its citizens keep, and spend as they please, some of their own money. Such devices will be thought of as "subsidies," and loftily denounced, especially by those whose livelihoods depend entirely on perpetual subsidization of the public schools, their pandemic problems, and their Byzantine and costly governance, as "handouts" of "public" money. Should credits or vouchers be provided by law, the same law would have to provide, as *quid pro quo* to a tremendous and noisy lobby of government employees, that most of the policies and practices that make the private schools what they are would suddenly become illegal. When private schools are required to hire certified graduates of state teacher academies, and to offer all the mandated mickeymousery of social adjustment disguised as "studies," and to make sure that the ninth-grade textbook for Appreciation of Alternative Lifestyles doesn't use any tenth-grade vocabulary words, then the erstwhile voucherites will long for the good old days, when you could at least get what you paid for, and when the private schools actually *were* an alternative to government education.

Those voucher and credit schemes were probably *not* cooked up by a conspiracy of educationists. Those people aren't that smart. But you just can't beat them for luck.

[V:2, February 1981]

Maximum Brain Dysfunction

EVERYBODY is in a whole lot of trouble. People all over America are losing their car keys and even forgetting their own telephone numbers, to say nothing of their zip codes. A man we know put an empty shredded wheat box in the refrigerator, and a lady in Tacoma asked her husband to pick up a tune of canna fish on his way home. Three out of four diners in the fanciest restaurants move their lips while figuring out fifteen percent of $48.83, and some of them will find that they *have* left home without it.

So what, you say? Ha! So you obviously don't know the first damned thing about minimal brain dysfunction, that's what. We *do* know the first damned thing about that dreaded disorder, and a supremely damnable thing it is: there are *at least* ninety-nine separate and distinct symptoms of minimal brain dysfunction! *You* are probably suffering from about thirty of them right now. And here's yet another damned thing: minimal brain dysfunction is itself only *one* of a whole host of "learning disabilities" that educationistic psychologists have somehow managed to discover in the last fifty years or more. And the damnedest thing of all is that when we ask those educationists why their victims are so ignorant and thoughtless, they say that they'll try to puzzle it out if we'll just give them more money, and we give them more money, and they hire each other as consultants, and the consultants duly discover yet another, hitherto unsuspected, learning disability.

So we were recently appalled, but hardly surprised, by a fat bundle of guidelines called "Michigan Special Education Rules." It is only *in theory* a separation of goats from sheep; *in practice* it is a charter of perpetual employment for goatherds. Its covert assumptions make the Doctrine

of Innate Depravity look like the sentimental dream of some bleeding-heart liberal, for the Doctrine of Universal Impairment has no counterpart of the Operation of Grace. It looks instead to the Implementation of Grants.

The Michigan Rules include: "R 340.1706 Determination of emotionally impaired." Stubborn neurotics that we are, we just couldn't resist the risk of self-knowledge that offers itself in *any* list of symptoms. Sure enough, the very first symptom of "emotionally impaired" was: *Inability to build or maintain satisfactory interpersonal relationships within the school environment.*

A double whammy! That is *precisely* the environment within which every member of our staff has plenty of trouble with those very relationships. Furthermore, since literacy has recently been discovered — within the school environment — to *include* lots of that interpersonal relation stuff, we had to find ourselves illiterate too!

Reeling with the shock of recognition, we managed to puzzle out, by lip-movement and subvocalization, the second symptom: *Inappropriate types of behavior or feelings under normal circumstances,* presumably still "within the school environment," although whether that is a "normal circumstance" is worth some thought.

A mystery. What *types* of behavior and feelings *are* there? Which circumstances are normal? Is it normal or not, under this very circumstance, to feel, as we in fact do, a feeling, if not a type of feeling, remarkably like another symptom of "emotionally impaired" in Michigan? *General pervasive mood of unhappiness or depression.*

So. When it's three o'clock in the morning of the dark night of the soul, don't go near the guidance office. There will be no waiting around for Godot in the hallways, no hesitation at the turning of the stair.

And the thought of all that "school environment" where all the little Donnies and Maries are all agog about Be All That You Can Be Week, and where "to be or not to be" is definitely *not* the question, brings on the fourth symptom of "emotionally impaired": *Tendency to develop physical symptoms or fears associated with school or personal problems.*

Right. Absolutely right. Bellyache and vertigo. And fear. Fear and trembling. The simple truth must out: We are emotionally impaired in Michigan. A classic case.

Who shall stand when the Impairment Inspector appeareth? Who shall abide the day of the Disability Determinator's coming? Not we, surely; and, whether out of some inappropriate feeling or this pervasive mood of depression, we're beginning to have some dark suspicions about you. We can see you, sitting there in some *appropriate* type of behavior, smugly congratulating yourself on all your swell interpersonal relations, and wallowing in your pervasive mood of jollity, without even a touch of heartburn. Well, just you read this little codicil to the Four Symptoms:

The term "emotionally impaired" also includes persons who, in addition to the above characteristics, exhibit maladaptive behaviors related to schizophrenia, autism, or similar disorders. The term "emotionally impaired" does not include persons who are socially maladjusted unless it is determined that such persons are emotionally impaired.

Well, at least you don't have to worry about being found emotionally impaired just because you're socially maladjusted, unless you *are* found emotionally impaired because of certain maladaptive behaviors that have brought you into your social maladjustment. When just about all of us are normally impaired, your sanctimonious unimpairment is about as maladaptive as you can get. And forget about trying

to convince us that those behaviors of yours are *not* related to schizophrenia or autism. Big deal. What about those "similar disorders"? Do you have any idea how many of them there *are*? All in all, you're damn lucky to be living in a country that still has to put up with all sorts of deviants. In some countries, those maladaptive behaviors related to similar disorders could get you shipped off to live in some very cold place where you'll probably end up eating your shoes.

It will not surprise regular readers that all this determining is done by members of the Affective Functionary Faction, government agents who keep watch over how people feel. In Michigan,

the emotionally impaired shall be determined through manifestation of behavioral problems primarily in the affective domain, which adversely affect the person's education to the extent that the person cannot profit from regular learning experiences. . . .

The wonderful thing about that Affective Domain, and what makes it both the Lotus Land and the Happy Hunting Ground of educationists and other pseudo-scientists, is that there is no Bureau of Weights and Measures in that fair land. To weigh, to count, and thus to find wanting, are the appropriate, normal, and profitably adaptive behaviors of those whose greasy thumbs are on the scale.

Cardinal Richelieu, who was a member of an Affective Functionary Faction in his time, knew how to determine maladaptive behaviors too. "If you give me six sentences written by the most innocent of men," he said, "I will find something in them with which to hang him." What can it mean for our times that a wily conniver of the bad old days suddenly sounds so refreshingly honest?

[VI:4, April 1982]

The I of the Beholder

I have now reigned above fifty years in victory and peace, beloved by my subjects, dreaded by my enemies, respected by my allies. Riches and honors, power and pleasure, have waited on my call, nor does any earthly blessing appear to be wanting for my felicity. I have diligently numbered the days of pure and genuine happiness which have fallen to my lot. They amount to fourteen.

— Abd-ar-Rahman III

You have no more right to consume happiness without producing it than to consume wealth without producing it.

— G. B. Shaw

Indeed, we all wish to be happy even when we live in such a way as to make happiness impossible.

— Saint Augustine

HERE are some excerpts from a questionnaire called "Perceptions of Sex Equity for Women Faculty at Virginia Tech":

This section relates to your general feelings of satisfaction with your personal work situation as a Virginia Tech faculty member. In terms of your personal situation at Virginia Tech, how satisfied are you that . . .

This section relates to your perceptions of bias against women faculty at the University and attempts to identify areas where inequities may exist. Do you feel that problems of bias against faculty women exist at Virginia Tech in the following areas . . .

This section relates to your feelings about the treatment that faculty women would receive if they voiced concern about sexual harassment or discrimination. Do you feel that women faculty at Virginia Tech would get a fair hearing on concerns about sexual harassment or discrimination in the following places . . .

Virginia Tech is an affirmative action employer. This section relates to your perceptions of the success of the various affirmative action efforts with respect to women faculty. How successful has Virginia Tech been at ensuring that . . .

This section relates to your feelings about the need for additional efforts to ensure equitable treatment for Virginia Tech women faculty. How desirable do you feel it is for Virginia Tech to commit resources to make additional efforts to . . .

We, too, sent out a questionnaire. The findings are enough to make a stone cry. Countless millions all over the face of the earth are accorded less admiration and respect than they feel they ought to have. There is no numbering the victims of injustice, from life's feast cast out, cruelly deprived of promotion and pay, and even of self-esteem. Whole legions are liked, but not *well* liked, and the endeavors of vast multitudes are not sufficiently appreciated. And everywhere, in each and every land and clime, people are unsatisfied, their potentials unmaximized, their self-images unenhanced. Alone in the dark, children weep, and some people are not entirely pleased with their personal work situations. What *is* this old world coming to? And what can we do to set it right?

Well, obviously, we need to set up a committee, which can draw up the guidelines for the establishment of a permanent commission, which will then formulate policy for the enactment of legislation, which will create a new department, which will mandate the existence of agencies and bureaus and offices, each and every one of which will send out questionnaires, which will remind everybody of how much there is to whine about, and will even offer some helpful hints to those few who foolishly imagine that they just don't have much to whine about. And then we'll need just one more little thing: a whole nation of people who are ignorant and gullible enough to answer the questionnaires. That part we can leave to the educationists.

We ordinarily suppose that philosophy doesn't count. We deem it not even a luxury toward which only the few aspire, but rather an aberration, with which only the few are afflicted.

But philosophy does count, even in the most practical matters, *especially* in the most practical matters. All we have to do to make people ignorant and gullible is persuade them into a silly epistemology. Then they can believe that belief is a way of knowing, that feeling and sentiment are knowledge, that any opinion is as good as any other, as long as it's sincere, of course, and that such speculations as these are of no practical use anyway, because, as everyone knows, philosophy doesn't count. People in that condition guarantee the continuance among us of astrologers and politicians and other pests almost as harmful. Ed.D. candidates and pollsters would also disappear if it weren't for the ready availability of those who will both offer and accept the uninformed and unexamined testimony of feelings and opinions.

And so, too, would the makers of "Perceptions of Sex Equity for Women Faculty at Virginia Tech."

The passages cited above are brief introductions to the sections of that document. Each is followed by an appropriate list of items to be weighed or selected or in some other way to be "perceived." At the end of the questionnaire, however, there is one last section without any introduction. It looks so naked and forlorn. The responder has

to answer *these* questions without any guidance whatsoever, without even the least hint as to what answers the
questioners most want. And these are *hard* questions, too.
Rank and serial number questions, questions of mere fact,
to be answered (by those who do choose to answer them)
for the sake of mere knowledge.

How refreshing and encouraging it would be to hear that
someone, somewhere, has sent out a questionnaire asking
for knowledge, for the facts, and for the evidence by which
those facts might be known to *anyone,* anyone at all, utterly without regard to anyone's feelings and perceptions.

It can't happen here.

One of the most effective illusions of our time is the
belief that our "educational" system is a branch of our
society. In fact, that system is the *root* of our society. We
are its creatures, and truly, since the great, central themes
of educationism are devised by agents of government,
children of the state. It was not from silly parents, or venal
hucksters, or from ignorant pals in the streets, that we
learned to prize feeling more than fact, and that mere
knowledge is only the "lowest level of outcomes," the first
baby step on the long journey to the land of the affective

domain, the realm ruled by awarenesses and attitudes, where the entertainers and persuaders flourish and govern, and where policy and law depend on the counting of perceptions.

Of "perceptions," an educationistic code-word for "feelings," there can be no end, and, even more important, no objective verification. Nor is there an end of persons who are less than perfectly happy in every respect. We can understand the Virginia Tech questionnaire, therefore, as a pretext for endless employment in soliciting subjective and anonymous testimony as to their emotions from interested witnesses about whose skills of thoughtful self-examination and temperamental propensities the questioner knows, and seeks to know, nothing.

We call that "research." And with its help, our social engineers, instructed by our educationists, who invented this kind of research by questionnaire, will, pretty soon now, bring in that bright new day when you won't even have to *pursue* happiness.

And if you have any perceptions or feelings in this matter, please try not to mention them where *they* can hear.

[VII:2, March 1983]

The Invers Proportin

". . . the ability to write well is inversly proportinate to salary.
. . . TV personalities who daily abuse the rules of grammar get
infinately more than English teachers."

THOSE, alas, and yet once more, are the words — absolutely *sic* — of a schoolteacher whining about low
pay and a bum rap. Why *do* they do it? They always end
up looking, like the striking teacher whose placard called
for "Descent Wages," overpaid and guilty as hell.

And, to look into *another* academic can of worms, here
is the complete — also *sic* — text of a letter *to* a teacher
from someone in the office of the superintendent of schools
in Cook County:

Please, show your transcripts to the Personal dept. and the will
advise you on procesure. If, any further questions please call are
office.

Although such examples are often sent directly to us by
readers, these two were sent in more or less *indirectly* by
readers. The first was cited, with appropriate comment, in
Newsday, in a serious, thoughtful column by Ilene Barth.
The other was used by Mike Royko (one of our favorites,
because he always calls a fool a fool) in a piece in the
Chicago Sun-Times.

Barth and Royko, like most newspaper people, are literate and rational, and, in many matters, well informed

and realistic. We are grateful to them for bringing such examples to a readership that is even larger — but surely not *infinately* larger — than ours, and we certainly don't want them to stop doing that. But they really ought to knock off all the deploring.

The trouble with journalists is that they lead very sheltered lives, never seeing anything more disgusting and horrible than corruption, rape, murder, war, and an occasional volcanic eruption. This is what gives them the amiable but naive optimism out of which they deem it useful to deplore the routine and firmly institutionalized ignorance in the schools.

On the other hand, every member of *our* editorial staff has spent an entire lifetime *in school,* in the very belly of the beast. We know there is no hope of reform. In fact, even to put an end to the letters that incense journalists would require nothing less than dissolution of the entire system that we call "public education."

It is only from a special point of view that "education" is a failure. As to *its own purposes,* it is an unqualified success. One of its purposes is to serve as a massive tax-supported jobs program for legions of not especially able or talented people. As social programs go, it's a good one. The pay isn't high, but the risk is low, the standards are lenient, entry is easy, and job security is still pretty good. By contrast with the teacher who wrote the letter, the uncouth "TV personality" is a daredevil entrepreneur working at a high altitude without a net. Should he commit the televisionistic equivalent of that pathetic letter, he would end up reading the midnight poultry market wrap-up in Lower Possum Trot. But nothing will happen to the teacher.

Regular readers might review our own long list of characters, all those decent, dull mediocrities, who work pretty hard to little avail. Pitiably ill-educated schoolteachers, and the ludicrous, drab professors of educationism who ill-educated them. Principals and superintendents sucked up from the least academic in a system where the merely academic is relegated to the most junior. The camp-followers of every kind, the facilitators, coordinators, consultants, who have jobs only because the system adopts causes and concocts programs that will *seem* to serve them. In a well and truly "reformed" education, what would happen to such folk? Do we want them out of the schools and onto the dole?

In fact, the system is perfect, except for one little detail. We must find a way to get the *children* out of it.

[VII:4, May 1983]

The King Canute Commission

If an unfriendly foreign power had attempted to impose on America the mediocre educational performance that exists today, we might well have viewed it as an act of war.

> *We have left undone those things which we ought to have done, and we have done those things which we ought not to have done, and there is no health in us.*

REAGAN was right. The rising tide lifts all the boats. And the rafts, too. And all of the flotsam and jetsam, as well, the drifting grapefruit skins and beer cans, and the rotting bodies of dead things.

Now, "a rising tide of mediocrity" has just been detected by some sort of national commission on something or other about the schools. Gosh, it's scary. Even the commission's report seems, if that first quotation above is typical, to have been washed ashore by that very tide. That broken English about imposing the performance that exists has an unpleasantly familiar sound. We suspect that a couple of cagey educationists wangled slots on that commission and imposed the performance that exists in the report.

The second quotation is *not* to be found in the commission's report, but it should be. In fact, it ought to have *been* the report. It says it all, and in much better English. And it has this further virtue, that it speaks in the first person, not of some hypothetically imposed performance, but of what *we* have done and left undone.

In the manner of the typical social studies text, which is likely to explain the Civil War by saying that "problems arose," the commission's report laments all sorts of bad things that are said to have "happened" in the schools. The commissioners are perturbed to notice that courses in physics and courses in bachelor living carry the same credit, but hardly the same enrollment, in most schools. That, as they must know, didn't just happen. Persons *did* it, and they did it by design and out of policy. And while *those* persons were doing that, and perpetrating countless similar outrages, *other* persons were standing around leaving undone those things which they ought to have done. Put them all together — you get *we*. And that includes every member of the commission.

To whom, then, do they speak? To them who brought us to this, in the fond hope that those miscreants are *now* willing to do the only thing they ever *could* have done to improve the schools, which would be to seek some other line of work? To the idle bystanders, who have known *all of this* for years, and who will now suddenly decide to do their duty and set everything right, an endeavor that can never succeed until all the bums have been thrown out?

Marching on Mediocrity

But there is no whisper in this report of the bums who must be thrown out if anything is to change. The sad state of the schools, which the commission aptly characterizes by its allusion to courses in bachelor living, is remarkably *less* sad for those vast legions of people who make livings from the fact that the deepest principles of American educationism do not merely *permit* but actually *require* courses in bachelor living, and other like travesties beyond counting. Such things were not smuggled in through the boiler-room in the dead of night. Commissions, committees, boards of "education," all approved them. Professors of education, who concocted such courses, commended them, and designed programs for "teaching" the "teaching" of them. Legislatures enacted them. Supervisors, developers, coordinators, facilitators, hastened into the service of every new empire and began at once the preparation of grant proposals for more of the same.

All those people, however some of them may have profited, were acting on principle, *the* explicit principle of American schooling for the last sixty years or so. It is, briefly and therefore all too simply, stated, the belief that *the* purpose of education is to bring about a certain kind of society, and that the individual benefits from education to the degree in which he is adjusted to that society. Combine that with educationistic epistemology in which mere knowledge is "the lowest level of learning outcomes,"* and you end up with what we have: the deliberate neglect of strict disciplines, which are not conducive to the persuasion and adjustment of students. Those bachelor living courses and all their siblings are not nasty growths on an otherwise healthy organism. They are the heart of the matter, and they will never go away unless the ideology that spawns them is specifically repudiated.

*See "The Master of Those Who Know" (page 71) for a consideration of the epistemology of educationism.

There is nothing even close to such a repudiation in the report. Taking pains to offend no one, the commission wags its finger in no discernible direction and never says what most needs saying: The trash must go! We must *stop* doing those things that we ought not to have done and do only those that we ought to do. The two cannot live together, for the bad will always drive out the good.

If it had said such things, however, the report would not have provided anyone with fresh ammunition in the Great War for Money. Good schools, stripped of all rubbish, would cost *less* money, but only the students would profit from such schools.

As only one of the many factions that make up the vast political entity we call "education," students have little clout. But all the *other* factions should be delighted by the report. It offers golden opportunities for academies of educationism, administrative bureaucracies, teachers' unions, purveyors and manufacturers of devices and materials, even guidance counsellors and change-agents.

Well, maybe they just did the best they could. We can hardly expect to achieve "excellence" without a little compromise, can we? And when "the best," the champions of excellence who lack all conviction, are sent out to do battle with "the worst," those thrusters and adjusters who are filled with passionate intensity, what else would they do but cut a deal? You wouldn't want anyone to get hurt in a squabble over *excellence*, would you?

[VII:3, April 1983]

VI

Mangled Language
(Elementary Division)

Sticht in the Eye

THE first thing you must learn, if you want to become a *professional* of education and earn big money from the taxpayers, is how to dream up cunning definitions for things that need no defining. As dull and stupid as that may seem, we urge you to persevere in its practice, for it is also the *last* thing you will have to learn. Many a splendid career in education has been built on nothing more than that one little skill, endlessly elaborated.

Of course, if you want *formal* training as a *professional*, we can only suggest that you keep checking the ads in match-book covers, but, if you're reasonably bright and willing to practice, you might be able to master this lucrative discipline/field/area in the privacy of your home. Here's how it works: If you persist in saying, for instance, that speaking is speaking, you can only be an unprofessional elitist. Your real *professional* says that speaking is "uttering in order to language." And what is uttering? Uttering is the "production of vocal sounds; i.e., sounds produced using the larynx and oral cavities."

Needless definitions are the natural breeding ground of silly neologisms. If you can come up with "to language," you can define *that* and sound even more *professional*. To language is "representation of conceptualizations by properly ordered sequences of signs; or the inverse process of understanding the conceptualizations underlying . . . sequences of signs produced by others." Now you trot out "auding," "listening to speech in order to language," provided, of course, that you have already defined listening as "selecting and attending to excitation in the auditory modality."

It's hard to believe that one educationist could do all that (and lots more) out of his own head, so we're guessing that Tom Sticht of the National Institute of Education spent plenty of time consulting what they call "the literature," a compendium of the inanities of other educationists. Sticht has bunched much such stuff into "The Basic Skills: A Frame of Reference," a "background paper" written at the behest of U.S. Commissioner of Education Ernest L. Boyer.

You'll be delighted to find that Sticht has selected and attended to excitation not only in the literacy modality but in the "oracy" and the "numeracy" modalities as well. You'll learn about the improvement of affiliations among linkages, and you'll meet the amazing BAPs* that go by the names of Hearing, Seeing, Motor Movement, and Cognitive. (Yes, he does think of Cognitive as a noun.)

If a man came to your door trying to peddle that kind of stuff, just how long would you aud his languaging before sneaking off to the telephone to call the wagon? If he told you that he had it in mind to do something or other to your children, something designed to affect their oracy, would it not seem good to you to provide him with a BAP in the oral cavities? Academic questions, to be sure. In fact, you bought all of this stuff long, long ago, and, although you have paid and paid, you will never be done with paying. Long, long ago, you gave your children to the peddlers to do with as they pleased. Now that the

*Basic Adaptive Processes.

children are more ignorant than ever, you turn, naturally, to government, which turns, naturally, back to the peddlers.

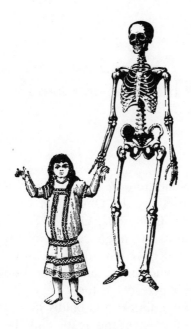

The Pavians, having given half their wealth to the Visigoths to defend their city against the Ostrogoths, and the remaining half to the Ostrogoths for like service against the Visigoths, found that they could no longer afford to live there, except, of course, as servants to the newly rich barbarians, all of whom turned out to be related.

[III:3, March 1979]

Eric Smeac's Practice-related Information Domain

THERE is something or other called ERIC/SMEAC.* It is harbored by the Ohio State University at 1200 Chambers Road, Columbus, Ohio 43212. ERIC/SMEAC sends out, or emits, we might say, an impenetrable annual newsletter, of which we have the issue of December 1978. It suggests (but who can be sure?) that this outfit is in the business of telling teachers (here called "educators") all about nifty new gimmicks and boldly innovative thrusts in the teaching of science and math and the pop pseudo-science, Environmental Education.† E/S is not at all ashamed to admit that it published *From Ought to Action in Environmental Education*.‡ Nor does it seek to deny its interest in some things it calls "information products" or that "a major effort of the clearinghouse is the production of a variety of information analysis products." The manufac-

*About ERIC we can't even guess. We do find this: "Clearinghouse for Science, Mathematics and Environmental Education." That's CSMEE. Maybe there really is an Eric Smeac, and this is just a part of his fiendish scheme to turn our brains into tapioca.

†Everyone has heard that those who can, do, and those who can't, teach. The adage says nothing about those who can neither do *nor* teach. For them, lest they vanish utterly from the public payroll, we devise non-courses usually called "educations."

‡This should be a dilly. It'll cost you three bucks, but it might be the funniest book of the year.

144

turers of gadgets and kits and "packets of materials" love ERIC/SMEAC.*

All of that we learn from Robert W. Howe, but other hands that might better have rested idle have also found work in this sheet. One of them tells us all about "the challenge confronting schools and colleges created by emerging energy realities." (Misplaced modifiers we can handle, but the thought of an emerging energy reality is just too scary. It could even be Godzilla.) The same hand calls teachers the "education clientele" and brings us word of "the development of adaption identification." Next we hear of "the Center's functional activities," a nasty thought, which include "maintaining access to a core [that's what it says: core] of personnel . . . so that programmatic aspects of the program thrust is appropriately coordinated." Well, those who are busy with important stuff like the appropriate coordination of the programmatic aspects of a program thrust certainly can't be bothered about trivia like appropriate coordination of plural subjects and plural verbs.

Worse is in store. This SMEACer speaks also of "new energy conservation supplemental curriculum materials focusing on the interrelationship of Energy, Environment, and Engagement." In educationistic prose, it is not a surprise when materials focus, but that stupendous noun pileup will call forth awe and envy in all *professionals* of education. That last bit, furthermore, is not entirely without wisdom, for many will surely testify to the curiously amiable interrelationship of energy, environment, and engagement, or something like it, at least.

At E/S they do things not when asked but "on a request basis." They promote phases, and one of their activities has conjured an effort. They do even better when they

---

*To those *professionals* of education who've heard tell of Newton, it's a mystery how in hell that man learned all that Physics and Math Education without so much as a remote-control film-strip projector.

write about some bureaucratic boondoggle called the National Education Practice File.

This "practice file" (their quotation marks) has "generated a variety of 'ideas' [*ditto*] within the practice-related information domain." (They do love a domain.)* And how were these "ideas" generated? They "were generated through group and individual contact with a variety of educators." Educators have principles, you know. They will never, for instance, do anything except as individuals or as groups. And they love contact, but again only with individuals or groups.

This newsletter reports that one Patricia Blosser, a SMEACer, went before a regional meeting of the NSTA. (That could stand for National Science Teachers' Association, but they probably wouldn't use the apostrophe.) There she presented a paper on "reading as a survival skill." We'd admire to have heard that. If the SMEACers know as much about reading as they do about writing, which seems inevitable, and if that paper was written no better than the rest of their stuff, reading it to an educated audience would have led to a demonstration of running like hell as a survival skill. The newsletter, however, does not suggest that Blosser barely escaped with her life, and that tells us something about those science teachers.

Of course, we could have guessed it from the newsletter. No one who cares about skill and accuracy could ever have written such shabby trash, and no one committed to disciplined intelligence could bear to read it. That the SMEACers do write it, and that science teachers do bear it, should disabuse us of the quaint notion that our science teachers have been trained in science.

No more would the math teachers seem to have been trained in mathematics, except, presumably, in the way

---

Domain is one of the darlingest weasel-words of the *professionals*. It sounds so noble. They need it, as they need *area*, *field*, and *sphere*, because we all giggle when they claim to know something about a *subject*.

that the teachers of Environmental Education are trained in environment, probably by hearing all about its importance often enough so that they reach a state of what the teacher-trainers would call enhanced environment awareness. Math and science have it in common that they are, before all else, habits of mind, and that they can find expression only in clear, conventionally correct utterance. Those incapable of such utterance cannot be teachers.

Well, who cares? With a little help from a core of personnel and a few file "ideas" from the practice-related domain, they can be educators. That's already a better job. Not too much work, automatic membership in a nifty education clientele, and no lifting.

[III:4, April 1979]

A Brief Note

We wondered how all those math and science "educators," presumably well trained in the skill of logic and the habit of accuracy, could bear to read the silly gabble in the ERIC/SMEAC newsletter. Now we know, for we've seen the work of Marlow Ediger, an actual math educator at Northeast Missouri State University. He warns, in *Wisconsin Teacher of Mathematics* (31:1, 18), that "the individual learner and society [will] ultimately reap consequential results." Like other educationists who refer to the subjects they don't teach in evasive euphemisms like "sphere," "field," and "area," Ediger speaks of "the mathematics arena."

If the editor of *WTM* isn't permanently out to lunch, then he's one hell of a great *agent provocateur* boring from within. Here's how he lets Ediger find enough rope:

Problematic situations must be life-like and real. Thus, relevant problems to be solved in the school-class setting must also have transfer values to societal settings. The mathematics curriculum then must not be separated from that deemed vital and relevant in society. If, for example, a classroom needs carpeting in the school setting, pupils with teacher guidance may determine the number of square feet or square yards needed. Metric measurements may also be utilized! Comparisons can be made for costs of diverse carpets from competing stores carrying the needed merchandise. Pupils in this situation are involved in identifying and solving a problem which integrates the goals of school and society. What is learned in the school-class setting is definitely useful in the larger society arena.

So much for the habit of accuracy and the skill of logic among math educators. Do you suppose there is, in mathematics, some flaw in procedure equivalent to redundancy? Is there some way, in an equation, to say that things are *definitely* equal? Is that weird exclamation point in fact a factorial sign? Is *utilized* to *used* as y' is to y, and the *school-class setting* some power of the *school setting*, itself some power of a mere school? Will multiplication cease in Missouri when all the classrooms are carpeted, or will the math educators, in some boldly innovative thrust, discover new problematic situations in the broom-closets?

Well, let's not be too hard on Ediger; maybe he just knows his audience. After all, he's remarkably specific about "stores carrying the needed merchandise," lest the hapless math educators go wandering into haberdasheries and bakeries asking about diverse carpets.

[III:5, May 1979]

Spinach

WE have been reluctant to take an editorial position on the vexatious question of sexism in language. It is true that language is both a display and a generator of attitudes and values, and that certain conventional devices of our language do suggest that our species is made up of men and special cases. (This suggestion is even more emphatic in languages that show gender in plural pronouns, so that the addition of one little boy to a band of a thousand Amazon marauders turns the whole pack into a masculine "they.") It is just as true, however, that most proposed remedies have been either illogical, ugly, or silly, and sometimes all three. What to do?

Now to our aid comes a faithful reader who has sent us the June 1980 issue of *The WS Quarterly*, a flacksheet all about the Wallingford-Swarthmore School District in Walingford, Pennsylvania. The only article in the issue is "Grade Repetition.............." (Those fourteen dots are *sic;* maybe they're symbolic?) The piece is said, perhaps with exceptionally fine editorial discrimination, to have been "prepared" by one Rose Alex, a "reading specialist" at large in the Wallingford Elementary School.

Rose Alex is a preparing specialist too. She has prepared her article in the form of a hypothetical (let's hope) conversation between a bewildered and remarkably unobservant parent and a confident, patient, knowledgeable reading specialist — a real pro. The pitiful parent asks questions like this:

My child's teacher has suggested that he/she not go on to the next grade this coming year, but repeat the grade. How can I be sure that repeating the grade is the best thing for my child?

Rose Alex replies, in part:

To try to make a child believe he/she is achieving by giving him/her tasks at a slower pace does not fool him/her when he/she sees his/her peers moving ahead of him/her.

That does it. We're ready to take a stand. We say it's spinach, and we say the hell with it.

[IV:7, October 1980]

The Lady with the Lump

I can stand out the war with any man.

Nightingale Clobbered! Sings no More

Intentionality of Consciousness Reported in Family Ecosystem

JUST when we thought we had it all figured out, just as we had *definitely* concluded ' that women would never indulge themselves in the ludicrous linguistic posturing so natural to men, we got some bad news from Akron. It came in these very words, and we are afraid that they *may* have been written by a *woman:*

Assumptions from theories of ecology and phenomenology provide an ecological-phenomenological perspective. The ecological-phenomenological perspective provides the framework for graduate education to prepare family health nurses to assist families in sustaining that quality of life which enables them to survive and prevail. From an ecological-phenomenological perspective the faculty views families within a macro-ecosystem, a meta-ecosystem, and a micro-ecosystem; and perceives the phenomena of the family ecosystem in terms of the intentionality of consciousness of enfamilied selves as reported by family members.

And there's more, lots more. And it's all the same, of course, except when it's worse. That "intentionality," for example, is later defined — well, not defined, but at least *viewed* — "viewed as those motives and goals that lead to expansions of consciousness." And consciousness is "viewed as five domains of living: valuing, thinking, feeling, acting, and intuiting."

Now you might suspect that when intentionality *does* lead to expansion of consciousness, it might, at least, open up a couple of new domains, loafing about and woolgathering, perhaps, but no. It turns out that "expansion of consciousness is viewed as a dialectical process which encompasses thesis of being, antithesis of doing and synthesis of becoming."

Heavy.

If all this puts you in mind of one of those real intellectual institution places where they figure the ontological isness of It All, it's only because you've forgotten — and who can blame you? — the key word in the cited passage: "nurses."

Yes, this is all about how they "teach" nurses something or other at the College of Nursing at the University of Akron.

Florence Nightingale said that she could stand out the war, and she did. She also said:

No *man*, not even a doctor, ever gives any other definition of what a nurse should be than this — "devoted and obedient." This definition would do just as well for a porter. It might even do for a horse.

Somehow, we don't think it cheers her to know that the *women* who are defining the nurse are *so* docile and obedient that they even want to talk like men, which no self-respecting horse would dream of.

[VI:5, May 1982]

VII

Quis Custodiet...

A Big "A" for Effort

The essential factor that keeps the scientific enterprise healthy is a shared respect for quality. Everybody can take pride in the quality of his own work, and we expect rough treatment from our colleagues whenever we produce something shoddy.

— The words of Freeman Dyson, a physicist,
in *The New Yorker*, August 6, 1979, page 40

WELL, sure, but let's be reasonable. There are, after all, enterprises in which rough treatment for shoddy work would be downright churlish. When your kids come home from camp, do you tell them that their pots are lumpy and leaky and their popsicle-stick pencil-holders all askew? Do you inform that sweet old lady who plays the harmonium at choir practice that her rhythm is uncertain and her accidentals accidental and that she'd do better playing on a touch-tone telephone? And how about that tap-dancing

at the junior high talent show, and the mimeographed newsletter your Aunt Tabiatha emits every Christmas?

Now, if you'll just give such things a little humanistic thought, maybe you can enhance your values on a holistic basis in the good old affective domain. Then, when your neighborhood principal sends out a page of ungrammatical babble, maybe you'll be sensitive enough to give him as much consideration as you give the baton twirlers in the homecoming parade. It's honest effort that counts, isn't it, and that principal is doing the best he can.

Those of us who have landed steady jobs in the schools understand these things, and we always give each other A

for effort, and never, *never*, any of that rough treatment stuff. When our colleagues undertake a modification of the sequencing of modules within clusters exposing students to a variety of experiences including module instruction in basic skills, do we mutter about a shared respect for quality? We do not. We know that that's the best they can do, and we give them A for effort. When the guy down the hall is teaching intercultural sensitivity enhancement through sampling the foods of many lands, do we fret about some utterly hypothetical distinction between academic study and those swell self-enrichment courses at the Y on Thursday nights? We do not. It's a shared respect for academic freedom that keeps *this* enterprise healthy, and if we find blintzes better than bibliographies and pizzas more to be prized than papers, that's academic freedom and none of your damn business, or any elitist physicist's either.

Physicists, you must realize, are unlikely to share those humanistic values inherent in things like experiential curriculum development and the making of collages from scraps of uncooked pasta. They have little appreciation of the noncognitive aspects, phases, and factors of observation-participation-involvement and painting on velvet.

So let's just restrict that "rough treatment" stuff to the physicists, OK? After all, those birds are *dangerous*. What *they* do might even have *consequences*, for God's sake!

[III:7, October 1979]

The Principal and the Interest

INSTITUTIONS feel no pain. Only people can feel the relentless pain of illiteracy, the desperate bafflement of a mind unskilled in the ways of logic and thoughtful attention, and dimly aware, but aware nevertheless, of its own confusion. Schools do not have minds; they have guidelines. Their guidelines run, when it isn't too inconvenient, as far as what they are not at all ashamed to call the parameters of basic minimum competency. Basic minimum competence (why *do* they need that *y?*) is not literacy. It is, however, just enough a counterfeit literacy to convince the minimally competent to fancy themselves literate, except, of course, for those moments of desperate pain.

And there is even worse in store for the pseudo-literate victim of the schools. As bad as it is, self-knowledge is better than public exposure. Imagine, if you can, the pain of a certain high school principal who now finds himself publicly humiliated and accused of incompetence because of an article he wrote, so innocently, for the school paper. Here are some excerpts:

The County office has coordinators in all areas that is willing to help when help is needed.

Every one who participated are to be commended for a job well done. We did not win as many senior games as we would have like too, but both teams showed excellent sportsmanship.

The Senior High band and the Junior High band were always there at the —— stadium when we need them. The Cheerleaders cheered the Drill Team performaned. The motivation and the momentous was there. It worked as clock word or a puzzle each part fell in place at the right time. If you were at the statium with me. I am sure you would have been satisfied with the performance.

The article also displayed some startling spelling errors, such as "surch" for "search" and even "intonative" for "innovative," and if there exists an educationist who can spell correctly only one word, the odds are seven to one that that word will be "innovative."

A dismayed parent, doing exactly what we have often urged, sent a copy of the principal's article, with appropriate commentary, to a local paper, and irate citizens petitioned the school board to remove the principal for incompetence. The superintendent said that he would "handle the matter as a personnel problem rather than in public." The resolution, if any, we do not know.

The principal further injured himself with defenses so pathetically irrelevant or implausible as to suggest even greater incompetence. He claimed that the piece was a hastily written rough draft, and that he expected that someone on the school paper would "edit" it. His errors, however, are characteristic not of haste but of ignorance; and few parents could have been consoled by his implicit admission that students on the school paper had higher standards, and would do their assignments more conscientiously, than the principal. The poor man put forth as evidence some other pieces he had written for the same paper, pieces in which his competence was demonstrated by "few errors" rather than many. He pointed out, as though the conventions of spelling, punctuation, and syntax appropriate to English prose were different from English prose *in newspapers*, that the education of principals does not require courses in journalism. And, most astonishingly of all, he further excused himself by telling the parents who had entrusted to him the intellectual instruction of their children that he was, after all, "an inexperienced writer."

An inexperienced writer. The man is a graduate of a small college, probably with a degree in education. He has a master's degree, probably in educational administration, from a state university. Can these distinctions, such as they are, be attained by an inexperienced writer? Did he write papers? A master's thesis? Did his teachers find no fault in his writing, or in his scholarship, which they could not possibly have assessed without reading what he had written?

And that school board that made him a principal and that now faces a nasty "personnel problem" too delicate to be "handled" in public, did it consider his academic and intellectual achievements? How did it measure them? Was that principal never a teacher? What could he have taught, who is so meagerly practiced in literacy?

Regular readers will have noticed that contrary to our usual practice we have not given the principal's name, or even the name of that stadium. We don't want you to care who he is, because this case is nastily vexed by the fact that he is black, and that the parents who seek his removal are white.

In one way, that is irrelevant. The academic and intellectual distinctions appropriate to a school principal are whatever they are, for principals of any color. And if such distinctions are *not* required of principals, which is generally the case, illiteracy and ignorance are no more to be accounted demerits in black principals than in the thousands of talentless gym and shop teachers who have wangled their ways through guidance counsellorship and curriculum facilitation to become white principals.

In other ways, however, this hapless principal's color is all too relevant. It permits him to claim, as he does, and perhaps even to believe, that the charges against him arise from racial hostility. And he may be right, which is *not* to say that the charges are groundless but only that hosts of white principals who deserve similar discomfiture remain unindicted. We're on the principal's side; we favor equal exposure and humiliation for *all* the ignoramuses who have been awarded, by virtue of silly degrees from academies of educationism, undemanding employment in the public school jobs program.

But we are *not* on his side when he says that "there are more people interested in the education of students than in this petty kind of bias." The blackness of the principal and the whiteness of his opponents are, for some purposes, not to the point, but the redness of that herring cannot be ignored. It is precisely in the cause of "the education of students" that we must object to academic deficiencies in principals of any color whatsoever. Furthermore, the principal's pathetic ploy makes us wonder: What notion of "education" does he harbor, in which the elementary mechanical skills of literacy are of so little importance? And, even worse, if he in fact believes that the ignorance of an inexperienced writer is being condemned only because the writer happens to be black, would he prefer that it be *excused* only because the writer is black?

No, the poor man simply has no legitimate defense. But he *does* have a legitimate complaint. Since he seems unlikely to think of it, and since almost all the rest of us can legitimately make the same complaint, we are going to make it.

That principal is suffering. The students, and their parents, are suffering. The whole town is suffering, and so is a whole nation, where fewer and fewer of those who call themselves "educators" have attained even the once standard level of mediocrity. But some people are not suffering. The teachers who handed that principal his high school diploma without having taught him even such simple things as spelling and punctuation (what *else* did they neglect?), they are not suffering. And the professors who took their pay from his tuition and gave him passing grades and a college degree and sent him forth as a certified educator and wrote warm letters of recommendation to graduate schools, all without knowing, or caring, that he was "an inexperienced writer" who couldn't even spell or punctuate correctly, they are not suffering. And the educationists who welcomed him (and his money) into the high calling of scholarship and pronounced him a "master" and in every way fit mentor of youth and who testified to his intellectual prowess and consummate learning to an unwary (and now unhappy) school board, they are not suffering.

The principal thinks himself educated. And why not? All those people *told* him that he was educated, and they gave him the papers to prove it. So what else can he believe now but that his troubles are the result of racial discrimination? And he may still be right.

Did all of those culprits pass him along because they didn't *know* his weakness? Bad. Because they didn't care? Worse. Or did they presume that his race would probably make superior intellectual achievement unlikely and would also protect him from the consequences of its absence? The worst. Beyond these three unsavory hypotheses, we just can't imagine any others.

[V:3, March 1981]

The Interest and the Principle

FROM time to time we find ourselves wondering why our traditional victims, almost always people with jobs in the school business and therefore at least mindful of the importance of education, write such terrible English. The obvious explanation just doesn't go far enough. While it is easy to see that they are poorly educated and often not very bright to begin with, that still leaves us to wonder why such people went into the school business at all, why the school business so readily accepted and nourished them, and why so little of the presumable influence of the intellectual life seems to have rubbed off on them. Now, thanks to George Orwell, we have a better explanation.

Consider first a few words from one William Paton, Superintendent of Schools in Oconomowoc, Wisconsin, in *Forward*, a fat pamphlet of education blather about "gifted/talented education" put out by the Wisconsin Association for Supervision and Curriculum Development. Paton, who laments "a dirth" of suitable teachers and hopes that someone will "give voice on a statewide basis," writes like this:

It is readily apparent that the major issue facing those of us concerned in this area deals with the question of how we shall provide equal and quality programming opportunities which respond to the needs of *all* children.

So. The merely apparent seems to be invisible to educationists, perhaps because they are always concerned in an area; they have to wait for the *readily* apparent. And the issue (*major*, naturally) deals with the question, the question of how. And what, exactly, are programming opportunities? Programs? Courses? Field trips? Or are they some improbable opportunities for the children to program some quality into an educational system run by grown-ups who can't make sense?

Well, who cares? Wait. Here's a better question. Who *doesn't* care? That we can answer. William Paton doesn't care. He's written his piece and probably listed it on his *vita* as a "scholarly publication," so why should he care that it makes no sense to say that the issue deals with the question? Big deal. And, while it is hard to believe that anyone except a penniless old mother would *read* an educationist's "scholarly publication," those others of Paton's ilk for whom the piece was intended won't care either. How can they? They are themselves quite concerned in areas where issues deal with questions.

In the essay "Politics and the English Language," his fullest exploration of the inevitable influences of thought and language upon one another, Orwell shows us how to understand *why* the Patons of Academe do what they do. He speaks of the writer who is unable to say what he means, the writer who inadvertently says what he does *not* mean, and the writer who, improbable as it seems, is not *interested* in what he is saying and who is therefore indifferent as to what he might mean. The first two suffer merely from incapacity, but it is that very incapacity that is engendered and sustained by the indifference of the third. The babblers of educationism write and think badly because they are not interested in education.

Can you detect in Paton's prose some impassioned concern for the intellectual nurture of those "gifted/talented" students, who are probably far more attentive and thoughtful than the bureaucrat who presumes to superintend them? Was it out of deep commitment to the value of clarity and precision in the work of the mind that Paton found the issue that deals with the question of how quite good enough for his purposes? What practiced discipline of the intellect, what love of learning, can we suppose in a man who will not even lift his pen a moment to consider what he means by "quality programming opportunities"? And if these are "little" things, shall we conclude from them that this busy superintendent will nevertheless give his powers of attentive thoughtfulness and meticulous workmanship to his superintendence of the big things — like education?

How can it be that people choose to spend their lives in a calling that interests them so little that they won't trouble themselves to make sense when thinking about it? Adam Smith answered that question long ago:

It is the interest of every man to live as much at his ease as he can; and if his emoluments are to be precisely the same, whether he does, or does not perform some very laborious duty, it is certainly his interest, at least as interest is vulgarly understood, either to neglect it altogether, or, if he is subject to some authority which will not suffer him to do this, to perform it in as careless and slovenly a manner as that authority will permit.

Where there is an inward commitment to the worth of knowledge and reason — not only because they are useful, but because they are good — the authority of principle is enough to ensure both the interest and the good workmanship that lead to clarity and precision, and even to grace, in statement. But the typical training of an educationist, which often begins with a skimpy, C minus undergraduate major and peters out with a "doctorate" in education, the highest rung on the ladder of social promotion, seems neither to require nor to foster such a commitment. If it did, they would not, they *could* not, write their habitual, inane gibberish.

And, as they lack the inward authority of principle, they lack also the supervision of outward authority. They have jobs in agencies of government, where people may sometimes be held accountable for some things, tardiness, perhaps, but never, *never*, for the quality of the work of their minds. In the entire, tremendous apparatus of public education, there is *no one* who will say, "Look here, Paton. This just won't do! Surely, the high calling that you have chosen, and which has, by the way, rewarded you rather handsomely, especially considering that with the devotion and ability that *this* stuff suggests you'd never be superintendent of *anything* in an outfit that had to show a profit, deserves more thoughtful attention and — yes, dammit! — *respect* than you have given it!"

But they have principals, not principles, in the public schools. So the legions of Patons will go on forever, securely enjobbed among the like-unminded, impervious to intellectual discipline, which isn't in their job descriptions, serving what does not interest them but is much in their interest, at least as interest is vulgarly understood.

[V:4, April 1981]

...And furthermore

Here's *another* superintendent of schools, Richard C. Hamilton, Ed.D., who superintends the love of learning and the growth of intellectual power among the youth of North Hampton, New Hampshire. He is a man, as the educationists say, very giving of self, and *perfectly willing* to lighten the darkness of grown-ups *too*, as he does in his latest annual report:

A new phrase has caught my ear and I would like to use it in discussing you, your children, and the ensuing relationship. The phrase is "centering down."

"Centering down" to me means a placing of one's interest in a central focus, a separating of the important and the not so important, mentally reducing things to a discernible entity.

Well, the darnedest things *will* catch the ear in a cold climate, but this one sounds really neat. Come on now, haven't you always *wanted* to reduce things to a discernible entity and all that other good stuff? And how about the meaning and purpose of *life?* That interest you any?

To "center down" in regard to our children is to me a putting into focus what we are here for.

Well, *sure* you want to learn to center down, and of *course* it's hard. It's positively *philosophical*. But don't you worry, bless your heart. You're going to have the unmitigated help of Richard C. Hamilton, Ed.D., and he's a *professional educator* who knows how to explain very complicated things even to the likes of you so that you can understand them right in the comfort of your *own home!* Ready? He-e-e-e-re he goes!

Have you "centered down" by climbing into a tent formed by the kitchen chairs and a blanket? Have you "centered down" by agreeing to put up with what goes with a puppy?

Now you get out there and center down and BOOGIE!

[V:4, April 1981]

The Great Iacono Flap

It has come to my attention that the announcement that I conveyed via the intercom the day following the Chester High–St. James basketball game which I disapproved of the loss. It was inferred, unfortunately, that I placed the reproach upon my coach. I wish to rectify that immediately.

CAN our schools ever hope to rise above their own principals? It seems unlikely. Consider for instance a certain A. N. Iacono, whose words, conveyed in this case via bulletin on December 12, 1980, you have just read. Iacono — Oops! We should have said *Doctor* Iacono. University of Pennsylvania, ya know. Fine old ivy league school. Real high standards. OK. *Doctor* Iacono is the principal of Chester High School in Chester, Pennsylvania. Here's the rest of his bulletin:

First, I had apologized to Mr. Wilson in the presence of Mr. White, Athletic Director, after the announcement for my error for which I maintain my innocence. Second, the following day, I made another announcement personally to Mr. Wilson explaining and apologizing for my actions. Third, I apologized to Mr. Wilson in the presence of Mr. Zyckowicz because of a grievance which was lodged. Fourth, I am apologizing to the faculty via my own volition and by no method a prompting from anyone because of those receivers of my announcement that perceived it as unprofessional.

I adhere to the dictum that professionalism must be maintained at all costs, and by no means would I thrust any aspect of our profession which may be construed as negative.

For the latter I abjectly apologize. However, I will continue to maintain my stance that I appreciate winning, and I want to be part of a winning team. This is by no means a reflection upon any individual but rather an indictment of my personality.

Yes. Well, we do agree, although we would prefer not to stick to a dictum, that "professionalism" should be "maintained," whatever that means. However, we find it hard to figure out exactly *what* profession it is of which *Doctor* Iacono will so prudently thrust by no means (or method) any aspect which may be construed as negative. Doctor Iacono signs himself "Principal," but the quality of his prose, which he apparently does *not* disapprove of the loss, suggests something less than the academic and intellectual excellence that we might have expected of a learned doctor and leader of youth in the ways of the life of the mind. In fact, if the basketball players of Chester High School can dribble and pass with twice the grace and precision, and love of excellence, with which their principal plays *his* little game, it's going to be one hell of a long season.

In spite of his lofty far-be-it-from-me tone, and precisely because of incompetence in language, the medium of thought, the hapless *Doctor* Iacono does manage to thrust some aspects of his "profession" that must be "construed as negative." His solecisms and gaucheries are outward and visible signs of certain inward and ideological aspects,* the very aspects that have foisted upon us schools

---

*Educationistic readers will find all this easier to understand by reminding themselves that an aspect might just as well be a facet. Or a factor. Or a component. Or whatever.

†But it may be that principals *don't* think of themselves as "academic" officers. A recent *Bulletin* of the Council for Basic Education quoted some school superintendent who apparently could see no irony at all in proclaiming himself "a leader in education except for curriculum." Those who automatically equate the money that is spent on the schools with "funding for education" would do well to consider the implications of those words.

whose chief academic officers† just can't make sense —
neither via intercom nor volition.

Buried in that ludicrous prose is the far from ludicrous
belief that incompetence, which *counts* in sport, *doesn't* count
in the mind. Doctor Iacono, an educationist who knows
that self-esteem is far more important than mere accuracy
and precision, blithely refers to his evidently garbled and
thoughtless announcement as "my error for which I maintain my innocence"!

Farther down, there is even a hint that the "error" may
have been no such thing at all. Doctor Iacono does make
it clear that if there *had* been any "prompting" it would
have been "because of those *receivers* of [his] announcement that *perceived* it as unprofessional." So there.

And there, in miniature, is the guiding ideology of educationism, an anti-intellectual, no-fault relativism, where
it just wouldn't be *fair* if mere errors had consequences,
and where the meaning of facts and events is not the object of thoughtful inquiry but rather a *sentiment* that some
receivers may perceive. It is only through consistent application of such principles that we get such principals,
who can neither dribble nor pass on paper, but who will
thrust no negative aspects and will bravely maintain their
stances that they appreciate winning.

[V:6, September 1981]

Sheer Doctoral Competence

High Order Acquisition Testimony to High-standard Endeavor where Seminars Plumb Assists

Awesomeness Partially Comprehended in Texas

YES, it's true. Only in Texas could it happen, and only Nolan Estes could have brought it off. It was Estes, as superintendent of schools in Dallas, who put an end to busing. With a single flap of his nimble tongue, he sent the children to school in motorized attendance modules. So we just *knew* that if there was *any* educationist who might partially comprehend the awesomeness of superintending, it would *have* to be good ol' Nolan.

He *says* so himself, in a real fine article we found in *Texas School Business*. (You won't find a sprightlier journal of thrusts from out on the cutting edge of the fast lane than good ol' *TSB*.) Estes's article, co-authored by one L. D. Haskew, who doesn't seem to have made any difference, is called "The Cooperative Superintendcy Program," but maybe that's a typo. It's really about some great superintend*en*cy program that Estes is running at the

University of Texas, where he has become a "Professor" and *also* an "Education Administrator," or maybe just a plain "Professor Education Administrator." From the way it's printed, it's hard to tell. Anyway, it's a swell job for an experienced flapper of tongue. Consider this:

Doctoral courses in Educational Administration focus on high-level superintending attainments (e.g. planmaking) as well as upon intellectual development (e.g. organization strategy for instruction) and sheer doctoral competence (e.g. research design, rational thinking). Seminars, called "Leadership Clinics," plumb the technological assists to constructive leaderly superintending. Dissertation design and production are high-standard endeavors which also focus upon a chosen facet of superintending's broad concerns. Flexibility in the hourly schedules for TEA work-assignment performance enhances competence-development by course engagements. The Fellows emerge with a University of Texas Ph. D. degree as testimony to high order professional and scholarly acquisitions.

How's that for sheer doctoral competence in high-standard endeavor?

It is entertaining, of course, to think of plumbing the assists and enhancing that "competence-development" by "course engagements." And we could provide you a titter by prowling through the piece and telling you that the elements abound with training, that performances will be factored into competencies, that far upness must escalate, and that there should be plenty of relational constructiveness with workmates. It might be fun to hear that when Estes and Haskew *say* "Artifacts from administrative/developmental performance," they don't mean, as one who knows both the meaning of "artifact" and the nature of educationistic labors might suppose, dried up ball-points, aeroplanes folded from memos, and paperclips malformed into projectiles. E. and H. mean, however, "newspaper clippings, citations or awards, pointed [?] letters of commendation, employee evaluation sheets." Or we might consider superintending itself, myriad in its demands, they say, and test whether we *too* — so naive that we can't even understand why people who *want* a Leadership Clinic don't just go and *have* one, instead of setting up a seminar and then *calling* it a Leadership Clinic — test whether *we* can hope to comprehend partially the awesomeness of superintending.

But this, unlike the esoteric *TSB*, is a humble little journal of simple ideas. It's as much as we can do to handle the easy stuff. Hyphens, for instance. Hyphens, in fact, can tell us all we need to know about sheer doctoral competence (e.g., rational thinking) in Texas.

These sheer "doctors" of educationism have as much trouble with little things as with big (e.g., rational thinking). They are *holistic,* and cannot waste attention on mere details, unless, of course, they have to do with expense allowances and fringe benefits. You must have noticed, in the cited passage, that the "high-level attainments" and "high-standard endeavors" suggest the tastes and habits of some environment other than Academe. "Now this here's your easy-clean high-standard chopper-dicer." But, more to the point, we are led to wonder about the "acquisitions" at the end of the paragraph. How come they're only "high order" instead of "high-order"? Is there, in fact, some significant (and intended) distinction between "high level" and "high-level," a distinction that the authors judiciously chose *not* to make in the case of "high order"? Is that absent hyphen simply a typo, which the authors, had they noticed it, would have taken pains to "correct" in the interests of clarity and precision, or out of mere sheer doctoral competence?

And what distinction do the hyphens clarify in "competence-development" and "work-assignment performance"? Is it the same in both cases? The former can only mean *the development of competence,* and that is what it would mean without the hyphen. But if the latter means *the assignment of work,* then the "Fellows" must be those who *perform* the *assignment* of the work rather than the work itself. So what the hell is it with these hyphens?

If you pay close attention to the sheer doctoral scribbles of educationists, and if you assume that unusual practice must serve some principle, you will understand why nothing can be done about schools. The people who manage them won't even pay attention to their own utterances, and they serve no coherent principles. See what principle you can derive from these forms, all from Estes and Haskew:

a post in top-management
elements-of-activity are set up
majority-choice is the exception
clinical-setting acquisition
positionally-prominent individuals
research and/or literature-synthesis

There. Now, if your work-assignment performance has been high-level, you will be smarting from office-insolence and in danger of mind-o'erthrowment.

[VI:5, May 1982]

VIII

The Making of
Teachers

Awareness Grows in Cincinnati!

WE'VE been reading this really neat sheet from Cincinnati. The public school system out there gladly subsidizes the life of the mind by setting its leading intellectuals up in a Department of Curriculum and Instruction, where they need never be troubled by the sight of an actual student. This leaves them free to think deep thoughts about new ways to share out the taxpayers' money, and to put out *The News from Planning and Development*, an esoteric journal of difficult ideas suitable for great minds. Most of it, naturally, is way over our head. It's heavy stuff, all about on-going interaction and models whose components are modules. Well, shoot, *we* can't even figure out how to devise the guidelines with which to pilot our parameters, which is, according to *TNFP&D* for July 1981, very *de rigueur* for something or other.

Even the easy parts are hard to grasp. Here's a piece of "Writing Improvement Project Funded":

The purpose of the training will be to make teachers aware of the substantial body of existing research concerning the teaching of writing, enable them to develop and implement a range of instructional material and writing activities for improving their students' composition skills, and provide them opportunities to practice these strategies in a classroom setting.

Subtle. And *professional. Real* professional. An ignorant amateur — someone like *you,* no doubt — would want those teachers to *know* what has been discovered in that "substantial body of existing research." (The body of *nonexisting* research is, of course, *insubstantial,* and thus slightly less likely to be funded.) The *professionals* know better. In the first place, as any fool can see, it doesn't *matter* what that "research" may or may not have come up with, since it obviously hasn't done the least damn bit of good. That's why these teachers don't know it *now.* Teacher academies have better things to do.

And that brings us to the second place: This is *school* business, and school business traffics in stuff much more important than mere knowledge. *Anybody* can find some knowledge, even without so much as a facilitator, to say nothing of a whole department of planning and development. Sometimes, even without *funding.* And knowledge without *awareness* is dangerously anti-humanistic; it may even lead to conclusions that suggest that it is madness to imagine that we need yet *more* "instructional material and writing activities" concocted by a workshop full of teacher academy graduates who have yet to be made *aware* of all that "research."

After things like awareness, development and implementation, and the practice of strategies, *professionals* prize most those collective exercises which, like cold baths for monks, dampen the anarchic flames of individualism. Now that the time has come for a few of Cincinnati's certified teacher academy graduates to try to learn how to write English, the *professionals* have provided that

teachers will participate in the composing process itself. They will write compositions and critique their writings the same way as their students would do the activities in their English classes. The rationale for this approach is that teachers must experience the writing process before they can successfully teach the process to their students. In other words, teachers of writing must write themselves.

Ah, the great Composing Process Itself! Always, like the wild dance of the quark, always going on *somewhere*. How wonderful to *participate* in it. Lucky, lucky teachers, to *experience* it. Such *awareness*. And lucky, too, that they will "do the activities" just as their students will do them, in the warm nest of participatory democracy, where any opinion (or awareness) is as good as any other, and where self-esteem runs no risk of injury in the hands of elitist authoritarianism armed with mere knowledge.

The blind, you see, *can* lead the blind, provided only that they all wander together in a dense mass. Only those few way out on the edges will fall into the ditch.

[V:8, November 1981]

Department of Gaga

When teachers in Santa Clara County get homesick for that scholarly life they came to know and love in teacher school, the local Dept. of Ed. is happy to provide them lots more of it, real neat stuff like this:

We will explore both theoretically and experimentially [*sic*] how to develop positive self-esteem in the classroom. We will create a positive and validating climate, in which we can relax, recharge and reinspire ourselves, and reaffirm our own essential self-worth and learn numerous classroom methods for facilitating positive self-esteem in our classrooms.

We will use such methods as guided imagery, positive focus, the language of responsibility, physical nurturance, communication recognition, strength identification, relaxation, and many others to help our students learn to accept themselves totally and learn to take action in the world. (Fee $30.00)

And here's a cheapy ($17) called "Science as a Verb," which it may *be* in their "language of responsibility":

Basic principles of science will be experienced through activities appropriate for classroom instruction; instruction will use common, easy-to-come-by materials.

How they experience principles, we don't know, but we'd sure like to see it, maybe just as they get to osmosis.

[VII:1, February 1983]

Voodoo Educology

Department of Temporal Plasticity

IT is a poet's luxury to sit around and wonder what the vintners buy one half so precious as the stuff they sell. For us, it is harsh necessity to discover what the school people learn one half so preposterous as the stuff they teach. It's not all that easy, for the stuff they learn usually turns out to be *twice* as preposterous as the stuff they teach.

We continue, nevertheless, to compile our Katalogue of Kollege Kredit Kourses, in which the following travesty is 4302.7Q. At the University of Bridgeport, however, the very same thing is advertised, to practicing and incipient schoolteachers, as a *course* in sensory awareness, worth three kollege kredits, and maybe a little raise:

This course is designed to increase the participant's ability to read, interpret, process, and respond to day-to-day sensory stimuli; to give participants a literacy in the many peripheral areas related to sensory perception and awareness; to prepare teachers to help their students expand the sensitivities of their eleven senses.

The above has been taught to high school seniors, to elementary and secondary school teachers, school psychologists, counselors, and social workers. The temporal plasticity of the course comes from its great material depth. This flexibility allows for an alteration of the subject profile to better fulfill objectives for participants.

We can explain some of that. The "great material depth" of this kourse comes from the fact that only the dead or deeply comatose suffer any shortage of "day-to-day sensory stimuli." The rest of us have quite a few. And we can, if we please, and if we can find a sap who will listen, natter about our stimuli. Since such nattering has the same value whether it persists for ten minutes or for ten weeks, those who persist in it enjoy the blessing of temporal plasticity. They can knock off early. And the instructor, who could also find something better to do, can always alter the subject profile so that the participants can get plenty of flexibility out of the temporal plasticity of material depth and drop in on the class only when they have some *really neat* sensory stimuli to interpret and process — good stuff from way out in the tenth sense, maybe.

Some of it we cannot explain. We do not, for instance, understand those areas, the peripheral ones that are said to be "related to sensory perception and awareness." We sort of wish that the person who cooked up that description had *named* maybe three or four of the areas he had in mind. We can't come up with a single one, and the more we try, the more our sensitivities seem to contract — in all eleven senses.

Nor is there any clue, as once there would have been, in the assertion that those mysterious areas are accessible to something called "literacy." This is, of course, the New Literacy, a far more democratic skill than the old, of which many innocents were deprived either by native ignorance or induced stupidity. To the New Literacy, which offers scads of neat options very much like Bridgeport University's peripheral area literacy, ignorance and stupidity are no impediments.

We found Sensory Awareness described, along with a full dozen other kourses of like ilk, in a brochure put out by a certain Redecision Institute for Transactional Analysis. (Analysis of the transaction in which the University of Bridgeport agreed to give graduate credit for these kourses is not provided.) RITA offers more lessons than Madame la Zonga. From her, if peripheral area literacy is not your bag, you can also learn: "using stroking as a major stimulus to human motivation"; "pupilometrics"; "techniques to establish and maintain rapport with students and elicit desirable responses"; and "strategies to produce behavioral changes in colleagues, peer group, couples, family, students, and parents."

Exactly what a teacher needs. No nonsense about math or literature or science — schoolteachers already know all that stuff — just a heady compound of Dale Carnegie and Dr. Goebbels. And all that for a lousy three hundred and sixty bucks a course.

In the old days, one of the day-to-day stimuli well known to teachers, and right in a peripheral area, was the sensory perception of sitting on a tack. Those old pros, without having taken a single course in sensory awareness, were nevertheless able to "read, interpret, process, and respond," frequently managing to expand a few student sensitivities at the same time. They had what we would now call a kind of natural tack-sitting literacy.

Nowadays, when the schoolteachers come, as the excellence commission puts it, "from the bottom quarter of graduating high-school and college students," we have to nurture in them what teachers seem once to have had by nature. So, if only they would use plenty of tacks, a kourse in sensory awareness would be right to the point. We could think of it as a way of sensitizing the bottom quarter.

[VII:4, May 1983]

The Glendower Glitch

WHEN our zany educationists call spirits from the vasty deep, the damned things actually *do* come. If you so much as whisper, within the hearing of one of those Porseffors of PedaGog/Magoggery, the dread name of Area-Awareness-Enhancement Modular On-site Methods/Devices, you can be sure that a year later you will find that very demon courted in classrooms and workshops required for certification. If you could name about four hundred such spooky spirits you could summon up a whole teacher-training academy. But don't do it. We have enough trouble now.

We were reminded of the awesome demonic power of educationistic wordplay while reading *The Official* Grapevine*. (That asterisk is *in* the title, and it leads to this: "Published for the Mounds View School District Staff," of Arden Hills, Minnesota. The *next* asterisk is ours.*) In an article called "Process Completed" we found:

Dennis Peterson, Assistant Superintendent of Instruction, has become one of 200 administrator perceiver specialists in the

---

*Luckily for the rest of us, the people who operate the schools are as noncognitive about our Constitution as they are about everything else. They don't know that the Fifth Amendment would excuse them from sending out all those silly newsletters and poopsheets. Well, their ignorance is our bliss, so we urge our readers to keep sending us that junk.

country as certified by the Selection Research Institute (SRI) of Lincoln, Nebraska.

The process toward certification, which Peterson began in 1978, was completed on Friday, November 14, at the conclusion of an "intensive" 2½ day training session held by the SRI in Hopkins. "The process and basic skills which the training develops are used mainly to identify strengths in potential and existing administrators and to focus on these strengths in future personal development," said Peterson.

See how easy it is? All you have to do is stand in the mystic diagram of existing aspects and potential parameters, swivel slowly for about two years ("intensively" for the final two and a half days), relating to felt needs and chanting aloud the subset of secret synonyms for the Great Perceiver, and behold — a mere and humble Assistant Superintendent of Instruction (surely he must be destined for better things than *that*) is robed in the greater glory of Administrator Perceiver Specialistship!

Ah, the life of the mind! Where else but in the schools could such wonders be worked? And just think of what the future must bring. *Quis percipiet ipsos perceptores?* By next year this time some canny necromancer will have conjured up that gaunt and grisly specter, nothing less than the Great *Perceiver* Perceiver Himself. Then, while Perceiver Specialist Peterson prowls the precincts of the principals, perceiving administrators, both existing and potential, hard on his heels follows the furtive figure of a former facilitator turned Perceiver Specialist Perceiver Specialist, perceiving Peterson's very perceivings, also both existing and potential. And *next* year . . . The mind reels. It even boggles a bit.

But the educationist dances and jigs. You get grants for that sort of thing in the education business, where it is presumed, and maybe with good reason, that only a certified perceiver can tell an industrious and effective administrator (there must be *some*) from an overbearing imbecile. In fact, any routine act of judgment performed habitually by millions and millions of only slightly observant citizens can become, if given a spooky name, a "skill" to be taught and eventually required. How, after all, can we trust the perceptions of one who has never taken *a single course* — not even one lousy workshop — in perceiving? And how can you expect a schoolteacher to relate to students without training in relating? Indeed, how can you even expect a teacher to answer a simple question in class without a thorough appreciation of the concept of microteaching in the classroom situation?

Microteaching. A potent demon. As it happens, we do understand microteaching. We've been reading all about it in an essay, or something, "Understanding Microteaching as a Concept," by one Robert J. Miltz, who admits that he is the director of the microteaching laboratory in the school of education at the University of Massachusetts. What it might *mean* to understand something "as a concept" rather than as some other thing, we do *not* understand, but the man says:

Most educators know microteaching as a scaled down encounter where a teacher teaches for a short period of time (5–10 minutes) to a small number of students (4–5), with the typical microteaching sessions including the teaching of a lesson and immediate supervisory and pupil feedback. This model has been useful over the years to demonstrate the concept of microteaching. The unfortunate aspect of this model is that it is usually interpreted as the *essence* of the microteaching concept, this interpretation has severely limited the use and development of microteaching. Microteaching, as a *concept,* is not simply a scaled down teaching encounter, it is much more.

There is nothing a laboratory director deplores more than an unfortunate aspect interpreted as an essence, especially when such an obtuse misinterpretation might severely limit the use and development of exactly that potion that he cooks up for the taxpayers, who already seem restless in Massachusetts. What *we* deplore is the failure to understand, as a concept, or even as a precept, the logical outrage of run-on sentences. But Miltz has better hope of remedy than we. We've just never been able to build up a market for coherent and conventional prose among the educationists, while they can easily sell one another (bills to the taxpayers) any old remnants or seconds they have lying around. Maybe it's packaging. Notice how astutely Miltz relabels his product, lest all the schoolteachers in Massachusetts tumble to the fact that they've been microteaching all their lives, by gum, and that it's no macrodeal:

What then is the microteaching concept? In its fullest sense the microteaching concept is an opportunity for a person or group of persons to present or develop something to another person or group and then take a look at what was done. This model opens up a wide range of possibilities not available in the more traditional model of microteaching.

There. That should do it. Now we can understand as a concept that almost anything, anything from football in Foxborough to a message from E. F. Hutton, is *really* just a form of microteaching, and that Miltz is about as far out on the cutting edge as you can hope to get.

But, of course, it's not to the point that *we* understand. The other educationists have to understand, and that, as Miltz obviously knows, requires reinforcement mediated by expectable parameters of learning disabilities in both individuals and groups:

First, unlike the traditional model, the definition does not limit microteaching to one person presenting information. There can be more than one.

Our definitive studies have shown that three out of five

educationists at least eighty-two times out of a hundred will, having carefully read that passage, exhibit certain behaviors that *may* be perceived, by some duly certified perceiver, as relevant to an appreciation of the concept of microteaching as a definition unlike a model limited to one person. That Miltz knows his audience.

Miltz takes the last "unfortunate aspect" of microcity out of microteaching by pointing out that "the idea that any size or type of group can be utilized as the receivers eliminates the belief that one must have only a small group of students." How true. And the idea that a pig could be called a cow and bread, cake would eliminate an unfortunate aspect of that tired old belief that if we had some ham we could have a ham sandwich if only we had some bread.

And bread *is* cake. Miltz makes that clear by telling us that "the idea of presenting or developing something frees the restriction that it must be a teaching lesson." And now, that captive restriction free at last, we understand as a concept that microteaching need be neither micro nor teaching. It need only be funded.

But there's one more thing. Feedback. Without videotaping machinery, which takes lots of funding, "it must be honestly stated that [microteaching] can't be done as effectively." So, whether we have "the holding of a problem session," or "an administrator [who] can gain useful insight into his effectiveness" even without the help of an administrator perceiver specialist, or even "a teacher who wants to investigate her relationship with a student on an individual basis," "for small groups or even larger [that should just about cover it] groups," "the real power and benefit comes from being able to actually see yourself doing something." And furthermore:

There is no restrictions [*sic*] on the way one receives feedback or the type of feedback one receives. It is simply stated that the person or persons have an opportunity to see themselves in action. . . . A person may look at the videotape alone, or with peers, or with an outside supervisor, or with students, or with any number of alternatives.

Well, we don't yet have our own microteaching laboratory here at Glassboro, but we have discovered that everything recommended by Miltz can be readily provided, contingent only on a little funding, at this really neat little motel just this side of Atlantic City. They've even been known to provide, *at no extra charge*, an occasional Microteaching Encounter Perceiver Specialist.

[V:1, January 1981]

The Sound of One Eraser Clapping

Every Monday I listen to sundry administrators lecturing the faculty on how we must employ the various aspects of curricular media to enhance the quality of education within the context of modern techniques and facilities. . . . The faculty is thinking of asking for nap rugs and milk during the films. . . . Burn this letter! If my principal finds it, she'll make me clap my own erasers for a week and cut my audio-visual access for a month.

YOU have just read excerpts from a poignant letter — nine pages, with footnotes — written to us by a public school teacher somewhere in the United States. That's all we are willing to tell you about him, except, of course, for his name. His name is Legion.

We get hundreds of letters like his every year from schoolteachers driven to frenzy by jargon-besotted, half-witted administrators, the officious noncombatants of the school war. You may recall the type. Twelve miles behind the lines, in neatly pressed uniforms, they drank fresh coffee and told you exactly how to enhance operational outcomes through implementation of alternative modes.

The teachers in the trenches are *not* educationists. Some of the least able do, of course, want to improve their lots by taking more education courses and becoming either junior assistant curriculum facilitators or teacher academy deans, whichever comes easier. Most of them, however, know all too well that the battle in the classroom is only with ignorance, a beatable foe, while the enemy back at headquarters is armed, intransigent stupidity, the vast, dead weight of established educationism, pavilioned in jargon and girded in cant. Even more than the children in their

classes, the teachers are victims of an institutionalized anti-intellectualism, dazed and ragged survivors of the values clarification concentration camp. Some children, therefore, will have the inestimable advantage of having for teachers resolute dissidents devoted to the pursuit of knowledge and the practice of thought, which depend absolutely on reading and writing.

Those who write to us, of course, are dissidents. We wish we could help them all. We wish we could print and disect all those documents they send us, the mindless maunderings of the ignoramuses who set standards and make policy in the schools. We wish we could tell every tale told us out of school, funny but excruciating accounts of that militant mickeymousery called teacher-training.* But we can't do it all. We do, however, have some advice and comfort for desperate dissidents.

Remember that you are not alone. The others are wait-

*Nevertheless, we do intend to print and circulate a little anthology of appalling anecdotes, anonymously or not, as contributors choose. Please keep sending them in. Stick to the facts — who, what, where, when. We have the other eraser.

ing for someone else. And even if they are slow to surface, remember that one working mind with a mimeograph machine can demoralize a whole platoon of superintendents and curriculum coordinators armed with bizarre mail-order doctorates.

Find that mimeograph machine, or make a deal with a friendly printer. Tell him Tom Paine sent you. The unspeakable acts of that rear echelon are detectable, as mental acts must be, *in language*, so publish abroad the very words, with brief, suitable comment, of those inane and

The In Basket

ignorant memos and directives. Comment *only* on the words, for which the public has paid, but do name the wordmonger. Leave batches of broadsides in the faculty lounge while your colleagues are unconscious, immersed in hair care and motorcycle magazines. You will be amazed at how far and fast the word will spread.

Go to the public, who pays you, remember, for the work of your mind. Take a lesson from a high school English teacher in Philadelphia, one Ronald James, who is willing and able to do the work of *his* mind on the editorial page of *The Bulletin*. Here is what he says, for instance, about some visitation by one of those HQ wonders:

The greater part of this specialist's presentation was devoted to providing teachers with . . . "accomodative strategies" for teaching students with reading and writing problems. He urged us to permit such students to "meet curricular objectives" (read: pass the course) with such "project activities" as charts, collages, mobiles, models and drawings. We were also instructed to provide our students with "alternative response modes" (read: don't insist that they write) including tape recording of lessons as well as oral tests.

One Ronald James, in one column, will tell more truth about the Basic Minimum Competence Hoax, or anything else, than the District Department of Information Services, busy "educating" the public, will disgorge in a decade. Go and do thou likewise. Pay no attention to your union, whining in chorus with administrators about the natural and proper appetite of the press for bad news about schools. Feed that appetite, and test your union's pious devotion to whatever it means by "quality" education.

At the very least, you can send a copy of this article to your favorite curriculum facilitator or superintendent of schools. He won't *understand* it very well, of course, but he will feel an enhanced awareness of doom.

[IV:8, November 1980]

The Ballons Nodule

CITIZENS out in the real world, usually but not always parents of schoolchildren, write to us complaining about the bozos who run the schools. The complainers often send evidence, which we are delighted to have, of course, but all too many of them go on to whine about their supposed helplessness and frustration. That puzzles us. We thought *every* American would know what to do with evidence of official malfeasance, even when, as in the case of the schools, the presumed protectors of the public interest are themselves the miscreants.

We have, for instance, a letter from an irate father in Wisconsin. Although he was relieved to learn that his son had not in fact been put into a nodule, he found that his tolerance of typos did not extend to big black caps:

A handout (of material, of course) was given to my son in his kindergarten class. It was a picture of a clown holding a bunch of ballons. I knew right away that they were ballons because the instructions on the top of the page said, "Color the Ballons." I had intended to send the original, but I can't bear to part with such a treasure.

And he asks, with this and other similar matters in mind, "What the hell should I do!!!!" (That's right: four !'s.)

Another irate parent sends *Update,* the newsletter of the Keystone Central School District in Lock Haven, Pennsylvania, where the molders of young minds say:

All incoming seventh grade students will be tested during the first two weeks of school in mathematics and english. The purpose of this testing is to find out at what competency level the students are functioning. This will allow the teachers to pinpoint specific weaknesses a student may have and help him to improve it during the year. In order to determine the progress a student may have made during the year, they will be tested again in June.

OK. Here's what you do. Do *not* bother going to the schools. The people who make policy there are ignorant or negligent or both. How do you think such things happen in the first place? Besides, the school people lose nothing when you complain and gain nothing when you approve; they get your money either way.

But *do* go to your local newspaper. With any luck at all, you'll find there a gnarled editor who once learned to diagram sentences, or a smartass young reporter fresh from the minimum competence circus. Newspapers don't get tax money, and juicy stories about ignorant educationists are happily popular just now. So strike while the irony is hot, or shut up and color your ballons.

[IV:9, December 1980]

Yet Another for the Gipper!

"SPORTS," as Heywood Hale Broun astutely observed, "do not build character. They reveal it." And that gives a new insight, perhaps, into Vince Lombardi's penetrating analysis of the fearful danger implicit in the academic enterprise: "A school without football is in danger of deteriorating into a medieval study hall." And that, of course, would be the end not only of American education as we know and love it but probably of the Hula Bowl as well.

Well, it's high time somebody just said it straight out, so here it is, ready or not, as the case may be: In spite of Roger Staubach's terrific grade-point average and Howard Cosell's truly awesome vocabulary, and in spite of all that the Pacific Ten and the Football Mothers of Wellsburg, West Virginia, have done to show their support for the American way of life, there still exists, in this great land of ours, a mean streak of *anti-athleticism*. And some of it, sad to relate, is *right in the schools*.

But don't you worry, because we can guarantee you that there's one place that *won't* deteriorate into some dreary study hall, not while Head Football Coach Paul S. Billiard is around. Now while we don't have the figures, we'd guess that Head Coach Billiard's Bruins at Brooke High School in Wellsburg must have some phenomenal record, for we *have* been privileged to read the coach's letter to the new football parents. He's a man who came to play, and right at the opening gun he tackles the dilemma of anti-athleticism by both horns:

Please impress upon [your son] that he is about to take a giant step in his young life, that of entering high school and participating in interscholastic athletics.

Now that's to lay it on the line, reveal character, and clarify values, all at once.

Coach Billiard has not, like some others we could name, knuckled under the mystique of intellectualism that still runs all too rampant even in some good high schools with very fine teams. Educator though he is, the coach does not flaunt his erudition around by talking over the heads of the parents and Football Mothers, which is just what happens all too often with guidance counsellors and curriculum facilitators and other such members of the higher-up intelligentsia in the public schools, who don't often seem to have the knack of finding easy words that laymen can understand. Even when he *has* to use the highly specialized technical language of the *professional* of education in order to describe something very subtle and complicated, Coach Billiard can find a way to make at least the gist of it clear to almost anyone of any educational level:

We have raised over $12,000 to help improve facilities in our strength room. Our strength facilities are second to none, but facilities must be facilitated (used).

You see? It *can* be done.

And, unlike some academics who always seem to think that *their* subjects are more important than any others, Coach Billiard recognizes that there's more to high school than just football. There may be basketball and baseball as well, and the coach favors the basics for any sport at all:

We are saying that the strength improvement phase is a very integral part of our total program. It is a fact that a stronger athlete is a better athlete regardless of what sport he is involved.

Athleticism, unlike such cold subjects as biology and algebra, teaches the warm human values. You don't see physicists patting each others' bottoms, and microbiologists don't even *have* awards banquets where they can express their gratitude to all the wonderful people who made it all possible. But in one sentence from Coach Billiard, a bright boy can learn some real human values that he might *never* pick up in your standard English course:

I would be remissed if I neglected to mention the outstanding cooperation and support that our program receives from our Principal . . .

Now can you imagine some math teacher writing to the parents of new students actually giving due and proper credit to the principal of the school for supporting the teaching of math? Probably not, because the people who end up teaching things like math, even if they aren't consciously anti-athleticists, do tend to be lacking in team-mindedness. They're off in their own little corners persuing esoteric special interests like history and literature.

Hardly anyone, of course, would deny that there is a place for such things in the high schools, especially for that certain kind of student. But we do have to remember that such studies do *not* tend to foster team-mindedness. Actually, they usually have the opposite effect. After all, we do have to admit that there is something basically self-ish and unsportsmanlike about learning such things as trigonometry or French. Those things may be all well and good for the person who learns them, but can you imagine what would happen to team spirit if all the players wanted to learn things only because of what was in it for them?

Furthermore, many of those subjects are unrealistically difficult, and even a very good player can find that the self-esteem that he loses in the French class doesn't always come back on the playing field. That's the sort of thing that brings on a bad attitude, the worst possible of all educational outcomes. And it is the Coach Billiards of this world, and not the teachers of French and trigonometry, who know exactly where bad attitudes come from and how to guard against them:

We discourage those individuals with poor attitudes to "shape up or ship out." A young man will not receive a bad attitude from participating in our system. If he is in trouble at home or elsewhere, his potential of carrying that characteristic into athletics is highly possible. Therefore, we are not about to base our program around individuals who are going to deter from the success of the team. (If the family can't handle the situation, don't complain when the coaches or school has to.)

And isn't that really *the* problem in so many of the non-athletic portions of a high school education, which are, in fact, based around individuals who do deter from the success of the team?

Coach Billiard hits the old nail right on the old head when he closes his letter with:

We hope that the preceding material has provided you with some needed information and supplied you with incite of the basic philosophy . . . of our program.

We'd like to believe that the parents were as incited as they should have been, but you know how parents are. Some of them don't even care who wins, so long as the kids are off the streets.

But if those parents will do just one little thing, there may be hope. Let them at least follow the advice in the coach's P.S.: "Please allow your son to read this letter so that all of us are speaking the same language." On that great day when we all speak the coach's language, there will be no detering from success whatever sport we are involved, and anti-athleticism will trouble us no more.

[IV:8, November 1980]

IX

Mangled Language
(Advanced Division)

The Porseffors of Eglinsh

PITY the Porseffors of Eglinsh, bearing through throngs of foes, of labourers and shop-boys, the chalice of sweet speech, language pure and undefiled. Dumb as old medallions, but not mute, they hear, in a place of disaffection, a grating roar of new men, other minds, hailing the only emperor, the emperor of ice cream. Ambiguities of seven sorts they understand, but from inservice aspects of remediation, shrink. Objective their correlative may be, and their fallacy pathetic, but parameters of inputs, outcomes, data-based transpersonal perceptions, they eschew. By rabble ringed, they stand and wait, bravely singing as they shine, but with so dull a cheer, their glitt'ring thoughts struck out at ev'ry line. You should have it so good.

So here's how they sing: "The latter poet, in his own final phase, already burdened by an imaginative solitude that is almost a solipsism, holds his own poem so open again to the precursor's work that at first we might believe the wheel has come full circle, and that we are back in the latter poet's flooded apprenticeship, before his strength began to assert itself in the revisionary ratios. But the poem is now *held* open to the precursor, where once it *was* open, and the uncanny effect is that the new poem's achievement makes it seem to us, not as though the precursor were writing it, but as though the latter poet himself had written the precursor's characteristic work."

Of course. "And," out of the revisionary ratios of a bailed-out apprenticeship, another self-precursing poet explains, "everyone will say, as you walk your mystic way, 'If this young man expresses himself in terms too deep for *me*, why what a very singularly deep young man this deep young man must be!' "

That turgid, pretentious prose, however, is not the work of a deep young man. It is the work of a mentor of deep young men. He is a distinguished scholar and Porseffor of Eglinsh at Yale University, a school in Connecticut. (We'd tell you his name if we could, of course, but the reader who sent in this example did not provide it. We have no way to discover it, either, since all members of our staff are forbidden to read *PMLA*, to say nothing of the insightful, trenchant, and seminal volumes of literary ruminations produced with no base thoughts of profit by the university presses. Let'm publish *and* perish, is what we say around here.)

Imagine, if you can, the contempt such a Porseffor must feel for a misplaced modifier. Conjure up his long exhalation as he averts his gaze, but delicately, from failure of agreement between subject and verb. Hear him pronounce, so subtly, the quotation marks by virtue of which he can say "feedback" with impunity.

We have said of the *Professionals* of Education that their language is inhuman and so all the more reprehensible in those who boast of their "humanistic" values. The inhuman language of the Porseffors of Eglinsh, loftily proud of their selfless devotion to the "humanities," is no less reprehensible. From the least intellectual inmates of Academe, we hear about catalytical non-disciplines facilitating us to move through a meta-transition. From the campus aristocrats we hear about imaginative solitude, probably to be distinguished from some imaginable imaginary solitude or perhaps from an imagined solitude — or both. Where the *Professional* twists our minds by centering his studies around, the Porseffor assaults our reason with an almost solipsism, no more understandable than an almost pregnancy. (Sure sounds neat, though, don't it?) He further asks us to accept — by faith alone, obviously, for nothing else would suffice — his oh-so-sensitive distinction between the poem now *held* open and the same poem when it merely *was* open. And, in the center of this pretentious mess, we find a shabby banality in that wheel coming full circle, just the kind of cheap cliché we might expect of the erstwhile wrestling coach who has taken a few courses at the local teacher academy and worked his way up to the rank of guidance counsellor.

Most of the barbarians who trouble these times can be easily identified by their native costumes — white belts, polyester double-knit leisure suits, sometimes even love beads. But the subtlest barbarian of all generally wears pure wool, a refined form of sheep's clothing. For pulling over eyes, wool has that polyester stuff beat all hollow.

[III:4, April 1979]

The Reformulation of Conceptualization

THE proposal from which the excerpt below is reprinted was submitted in March of 1980 to a certain
Society for Research in Child Development, as to which
we can tell you nothing more than its ominous name. To
speak of children as "developing" is to reveal a nasty in-
sensitivity both to language and to children. Complica-
tions develop, and images, but children learn. Or they
would, if we gave as much time and effort to teaching
them as we do to the profitable business of establishing
societies and soliciting grants for the study of their development.

There are surely no Americans who are just now in greater
need of good teaching than those "minority status children" to the study of whose development this proposal
claims to address itself. Must that teaching — and must
their learning — wait upon the "findings," probably the
"definitive findings," of some people who are unable to
make their verbs and subjects agree? Will the stupefying
disadvantages against which such hapless children must
struggle daily be somehow mitigated by the discoveries of
self-appointed savants who seem to suppose that "multiple" is a classy synonym for "many"? What can they understand or help others to understand who cannot see the

absurdity of "a comprehensive perspective," the logical equivalent of an extensive point? When the formulators of conceptualizations go on to *reformulate* their conceptualizations, what, exactly, will they have done?

The cited passage is not anomalous. It is typical of the entire proposal, which is characterized not only by frequent errors in grammar and punctuation but, much worse, by mind-twisting absurdities born of tormented syntax, and what can only be a ritual recitation of unexamined jargon. The proposal, which awards itself the distinction of being "*new* and *exciting*," and offers to "do . . . developmental and ecological views," promises to do them "while concurrently focusing (although indirectly) on historical influences which impact differentially the contextual experiences of minority group children who live in a majority group culture."

(Those children are called, apparently in hope not of precise distinction but only of stylish variation, sometimes "minority group children," or sometimes "minority status children," and occasionally mere "minority children." Fortunately for the sanity of us all, the proposers seem not to have noticed the possibility of naming those *other* children, whose curious and unaccountable existence they must have had in mind in that last part: the minority group children who *don't* live in a majority group culture.)

If you were a ninth-grade composition teacher charged with the education of a student who had written that passage, what would you do? Where would you begin? Would it seem at all to the point simply to *tell* him that *differentially* does not mean *in different ways*, or that *while* and *concurrently* add up to redundancy? Do you think he would take much profit from a discussion of the contradiction in his intention to "focus indirectly"? And could you hope to convince him that *impact*, especially as a transitive verb, has lost its force through too much use in the trendy jar-

An excerpt from:

The Social and Affective Development of Minority Status Children

A Proposal submitted by: Margaret Beale Spencer, Ph. D., Emory University; Geraldine Kearse Brookins, Ph. D., Jackson State University; and Walter Recharde Allen, Ph. D., University of Michigan.

The multiple issues raised suggests that a particular type of *structure* and *composition* for the study group is required. Thus, the accomplishment of the aforementioned aims require that the meeting be from a more *comprehensive perspective*. It is viewed as appropriate, in fact imperative, to conduct the study group conference in a "stepwise" fashion by holding two sessions over the extended period of time thus allowing adequate time between meetings to distill ideas and reformulate conceptualizations.

gon of grant proposals? What could you do to make clear to such a mind what is wrong with "contextual experiences," of which he is very, very proud?

Forget it. What that writer needs is not a lesson in this and that, not a handbook of helpful hints, but *an education*, a mind raised up in the habit of literacy and *the* skill (it is one and the same thing) of language and thought.

What happened to this proposal, we don't know. It was probably funded by that Society for Research in Child Development, or by some similar outfit, which will now point with pride to its mighty good works. Furthermore, the givers of such grants can rarely be distinguished from the takers, and they are ordinarily quite impressed by things like contextual experiences and the reformulation of conceptualizations. And anyway, it's not *their* money. It's yours.

Spencer and Brookins teach psychology, Allen, sociology. They may be "minority status" grown-ups themselves. (Do you suppose that *they* will be pleased to be so designated?) And, if they are, they are the only "minority status" citizens in the land who will take any profit from the funding of this proposal, which *will* impact differentially on *their* contextual experiences, but won't be what they need.

[V:1, January 1981]

Strangers in Paradigms,
or, The Hegemony Connection

WE are not guilty of omitting capital letters in the title of the passage reprinted below. Nor is that omission to be accounted, strictly speaking, an "error," except, of course, in taste. It is merely an example of what is known to printers as "cockroach typography," an affectation once thought more appropriate in ads for emporia devoted to the swift removal of unsightly hair than to the announcement of scholarly colloquia on the "richness — past, present, *and* future — of our collective humanistic treasury."

Cockroach typography is named after archy, that courageous cummings of cockroaches, who had to write his poetry by diving headfirst onto the typewriter keys, but could not manage the shift. And had the describer of "the paradigm exchange" been required to compose his piece in the same way, Earth would be more fair.

the paradigm exchange took place not, as you might well imagine, at Checkpoint Charlie in a murky fog, but at the University of Minnesota in a murky fog. It might not have been, however, quite the innocent romp it seems. Indeed, our staff cryptanalyst has concluded that the colloquium was nothing less than a "cover" for a covert operation laid on by a band of royalty-rich humanities professors in collusion with the international banking and fund-laundering cartel. In support of his hypothesis, he contends that the cited passage is obviously in code, which he unravels thus: "Taking stock. Capitalize currency exchanges [and/or] brokerages. Coin bank deposits richness treasury."

Well, while we do admit that an international conspiracy of professors and bankers is certainly more plausible than a brokerage characterized by exchanges of tools and explorations of modes, and than the examination of forms (*and* the paradigms themselves) through the application of modes; and while it is true that the supposedly decoded message makes a bit more sense than the original text, we're just not buying it. Those folk are *intellectuals*, dammit! They aren't even a pack of educationists, never mind international conspirators. We're going to give them the benefit of the doubt and assure you that there is probably nothing more sinister in that passage than a muddled and inappropriate metaphor, some vainglorious but routine jargon, and perhaps a pervasive malaise compounded of pretentiousness and the perfectly justifiable fear of academicians that no one out in the world is taking them seriously.

But the cryptanalyst remains unconvinced. He smugly points out that this so-called paradigm exchange provides a morning session called "*Accounting* for the Disciplines" (*his* italics), and then an afternoon session, "*More* Accounting for the Disciplines" (ditto). We reply that disciplines do indeed seem to require lots of accounting for, especially those that might be brokered through papers about "Modes of Space and Interiority: Ontology or Sociology," "Proust's Paradigm: A Production, a Figure, an Object of Reading," to say nothing of " 'Sociality' and 'Historicity' as Categories in Literary Reception" and the "Hegemony of Interpretation."

That was the point that convinced our stubborn decoder. He finally had to admit that no self-respecting gang of hard-eyed money manipulators and bagmen would take the risk of doing business with bozos who run so easily off at the mouth. Only a public institution of higher learning can take a chance like that.

So, thank goodness, the paradigm exchange was probably just a harmless frolic of porseffors. And why not? If the poets are to be the unacknowledged legislators of the world, they will surely need some help, some bureaucrats and appliers of analytical models, some paperpushers and methodologists of analysis and interpretation. Those artist types are clever enough in their own little specialties, but you can't expect them to handle the hard stuff. For that you need porseffors.

It happened once that archy's boss, Don Marquis, invited the insect to visit him at home, provided only that he come without any friends or kinfolk. To that, the Villon of vermin replied:

> boss
> you should have learned
> by this time
> that literature
>   makes strange
> bedfellows

So where is that cockroach, now that we need him?

[V:2, February 1981]

the paradigm exchange

Taking stock of the state of critical inquiry in the humanities and arts, this colloquium capitalizes on the diversity among the disciplines, and the currency of creative theories and methodologies of textual analysis and interpretation that bring changing perspectives to scholars and students. Exchanges of texts and tools and explorations of new modes of humanistic thinking characterize the brokerage of the colloquium. Through application of numerous analytical models, a variety of art forms will be examined. This will be followed by an examination of the paradigms themselves, coined in realms that bank deposits from anthropology, physics, history, and linguistics, to literature, philosophy, sociology, and psychology. The Colloquium aims to inventory the richness — past, present, and future — of our collective humanistic treasury.

Respeak in Monmouth

I am pleased to inform you that the Basic Skills Center is henceforth, to be known as the Center for Developmental Education. Dr. Andreach, Coordinator of the Basic Skill Center will be known as Coordinator of Developmental Education. Increasingly, colleges are dropping the basic skills connotation that goes with the kind of center we have established and are looking to the developmental aspects since they have more of a positive connotation than do basic skills.

WE keep watching for harbingers of 1984. The job is a cinch. Our maps bristle with pins, and we have often discovered readings as high as 9.7 on the logograph recorder. All the outlying stations report the same thing, and all the instruments agree. Just before the end, we will try to send out one last signal; but, should something go wrong, you may have to do that for us. We suggest: "The lights in the sky are stars."

We once brought you the news that literacy had become "a feeling of self worth and importance, and respect for an appreciation and understanding of other people and cultures." Just a few days ago, we heard from a mole at the Department of Education, soon to be retreaded as the Ministry of Truth. The DOE, we were told, no longer harbors any of those "change-agents," who had come to be looked on, by uninformed but noisy critics who proved impervious to re-education, as intrusive social manipulators. The change-agents, having passed through a larval stage as facilitators, have now emerged as linkers. Linkers, along with programs for linker-training and linkage enhancement will soon hatch out in every teacher academy in America.

Now we have the announcement quoted above. It is the work, the *deed*, one might better say, of one Samuel H. Magill, who is currently known as the president of Monmouth College in West Long Branch, New Jersey. We would like to admire his brass, for he says right out a shabby truth that most educationists would rather not tell. We suspect, however, that it was not out of brass but simply out of thoughtlessness that he gave away such an important trade secret. His use of commas is not characteristic of a cunning contriver, and his notion that connotations can be "dropped" at will is more likely a result of ignorance than of arrogance.

Nevertheless, he achieves the intended goal. Respeak takes its power from the fact that most people are not inclined to discriminate between what something *does* or *is* and what it is *known as*. Any educationistic enterprise can instantly win favor and support by giving its centers and coordinators, or anything else, fresh new outfits of the latest designer fashions in sheep's clothing. And the educationistic establishment takes from its own Respeak a double advantage. It can go on forever inculcating whatever combination of meager skills and pop notions it chooses to call "literacy," and it can thus assure itself an endless supply of those very people who are not inclined to discriminate between what something *does* or *is* and what it is *known as*.

It's a neat racket, and it would be horrible enough if it were operated by a pack of hard-eyed villains who knew exactly what they were doing. The truth, however, is even more horrible.

There *are*, of course, some villains. There are agency-spawned educrats and grant-hustlers who really *do* profit from "increased spending." There are book and gadget boosters who make big bucks from innovative thrusts. And there are even some supreme villains, ideological rather than venal, who want to fashion society to suit their ideologies. But those are just a few of the big kids playing hardball. Samuel H. Magill is not in that game.

The Magills of educationism, in all their thousands, are not villains. They are just modules, plugged into openings here and there. Any one will do. It's the *function of a component* that is needed, not the judgment of a mind. It doesn't matter whether Magill understands what he says. It matters only that he who is currently known as the president say it. It is the greatest triumph of our schools that they fit their victims to become their agents.

"All machines," wrote Thoreau, "have their friction. But when the friction comes to have its machine, let us not have such a machine any longer."

[VI:3, March 1982]

They Also Serve Who Only Look
for Work

THIS isn't going to be easy, so try to pay attention. We are about to quote from a poopsheet (what a splendid term!) called *Bulletin on Public Relations and Development for Colleges and Universities*. The *Bulletin* is quoting, with approbation, Ivan E. Frick, president of Elmhurst College in Elmhurst, Illinois. Frick will be quoting, also with approbation, Cohen and March, who must be members of the educationistic-administrative mutual approbation complex. Here we go:

Presidential leadership is always needed to get a college of any size to move and that task is seldom easy. Cohen and March did a study of leadership among college presidents and developed a theory . . . they called "organized anarchy." They said:

> An organization is a collection of choices looking for problems, issues and feelings looking for decision situations in which they might be aired, solutions looking for issues to which there might be answers, and decision makers looking for work.

There is considerable truth in this. An example is when one prepares a case statement for a capital drive. Establishing the case is not a simple process; its path is not linear, that is a straight line from one agreement to the next one. The process is always filled with a tremendous amount of ambiguity.

It is kind of Frick to explain the meaning of "linear," although his explanation does leave us to wonder whether that path from one agreement to the next might perhaps be a *crooked* line. But a crooked line is still a line, and so Frick must be saying that there is no line of *any* kind that leads from one agreement to the next. That would certainly make sense, allowing for a tremendous amount of ambiguity, of course, to anyone who has ever noticed the doings of educationistic administrators, but it's unusual for a college president to put it in writing.

And it's kind of Frick — ah, what a teacher he must have been before he was dragged from the classroom into the the thankless prominence of presidency — to provide us an honest-to-goodness *example* to help us understand that "considerable truth" in Cohen and March. We do have to confess that the really heavy thinkers, like Heidegger and Cohen and Hegel and March, are way over our heads. If it weren't for Frick's illuminating example, we would probably *never* have been able to understand why solutions would *want* to go looking for issues that might already have perfectly good answers of their own, unless they (the solutions) wanted, most uncharitably, and, one might well say in this context, quite contrary to accepted principles of academic collegiality, to replace them (the answers) with themselves (the solutions), thus leaving them (the answers) nothing more than disembodied shades flitting through the gloomy nether world of decision situations, looking for whatever issues the solutions might have spurned, because they (the issues) were *not* the kind to which there might be answers, the very kind for which they (the solutions) are looking. We wouldn't even have been able to figure out whether those issues for which solutions are looking are the very issues that are themselves looking, along with feelings, for decision situations. But now, thanks to Frick, everything is perfectly clear. Only a bona fide college president, by gosh, could have detected and revealed that much considerable truth.

Ivan Frick is not the only college president quoted by the *Bulletin on etc. etc.* (You can get your own copy, if you like, from Gonser Gerber Tinker Stuhr [whatever that, or they, may be], 105 W. Madison, Chicago 60602.) We also get to hear from Dan C. Johnson, of Mount St. Clare College in Clinton, Iowa. He tells us that "there are few, if any, institutional activities which cannot be enhanced by presidential presence."

Yeah, sure. The enhancing presidential presence. Let us be thankful that classroom teaching is at the bottom of any administrator's list of "institutional activities" and thus the least likely to be enhanced by the presidential presence.

[VI:4, April 1982]

Decision Makers Looking for Work

Missing Linker?

SPEAKING of decision makers looking for work, we suspect that we have discovered a genuine linker, one of those erstwhile change-agents turned ex-facilitators about whom we warned you. He is Terry McHenry, whose title would make a Byzantine emperor's favorite eunuch sob with envy. McHenry is Assistant Superintendent for Business Services for the County Office of Education in Santa Clara County, California.

Right at the top of its front page, the "Superintendent's Bulletin" admits that McHenry has completed "the extensive nine-month Sloan Program offered by the Stanford School of Business." (For educationists, anything that can be knocked off with a little inservicing is *in*tensive; if it takes a little more time, and a lot more money, they call it *ex*tensive.) Now, McHenry "has taken on the added responsibility of coordinating all planning," and "he will be using the techniques learned at Stanford and applying it [*sic*] to marketing and managing the various services districts require."

Well. Of course. We do have some grasp of planning coordination, which involves *not* mere planning, but the far subtler arts of planning to plan, and planning *whether* to plan. That might be what Cohen and March should have meant by "issues and feelings looking for decision situations in which they might be aired." But the rest of it is murky. What does one *do* when he manages a "service districts require"? Does he order paper towels according to those techniques learned at Stanford? Is it appropriate for the employee who *manages* services, whatever that might mean, to *market* them as well? And to what, exactly, is this mysterious responsibility added? In short, what does this man do for a living?

Fortunately, we need not speculate. McHenry describes his labors in the cause of the life of the mind:

Districts are our clients. Under the new planning program, we will hopefully do a better job of determining what the needs are in the field and, given, how we can meet those district needs.

This will be a lot more than just asking a simple question of do you want a certain kind of service, which is what they (the districts) have been asked before. It is a matter of what is the potential, and, what is the possibility of getting resources for it — either from the County Office or from some other source. We will be looking at the whole scenario.

We are going to start doing an overall look. The first year is not going to be extensive, but we have to find out what the attitudes are out there for the need and provision of services. It will be much more than a needs assessment.

Aha! The whole scenario. The potential. The resources *for* the potential. More, much more, than a mere needs assessment. But gently! Nothing extensive. The needs in the field will keep. First you have to *start* to find out those *attitudes* out there, the attitudes *for* need and provision. (Could there be any *against?*) Not an easy job. Might take years. *None* of them extensive.

So what did we tell you? The man must be a linker!

Please don't laugh at a linker. Without linkers there couldn't be any county superintendents, who can hardly be expected to superintend the *district* superintendents all by themselves. And *those* superintendents need linkers, both to link with the county linkers and to look at the whole scenario in superintending the attitudes for need and provision among the principals and *their* linkers. And *all* of those people need offices, and secretaries, and Mr. Coffee machines. Quality education doesn't come cheap, y'know.

[VI:4, April 1982]

Camera Obscura

My photographs establish the iconic, dramatic and psychological roles of contemporary high fashion photography. In other words, my intent is to identify the signifier, while eliminating the signified, . . . simultaneously creating an independent "work."

Wovon man nicht sprechen kann, darüber muss man schweigen.

WITTGENSTEIN probably had something much subtler in mind when he came up with that famous line, but the only translation we can manage just now is: If you don't know what the hell you're talking about, maybe you ought to keep your trap shut.

Not bad for a logical positivist, eh? But there is another and far zippier school of, well, not exactly "thought," but of something, surely, in which the counterpart of W's Proposition Seven reads: You got to I-DEN--tify the Signifier, E-LIM--inate the Signified, don't mess with Mr. Inbetween.

In schools, this persuasion has provided us Intrapersonal Appreciation through Holistic Writing, a form of Primal Screed Therapy in which the student lets it all hang out and the teacher pronounces it all peachy. In art, it has brought us what is so insignificantly expressed (which is *the* way to do it) in the passage above: that nouvelle vague of Gaga, Son of Dada.

That utterance is the "work" (and we joyfully endorse the iconic role of her quotation marks) of one Vikky Alexander, a photographer, some of whose "works" were among those to be seen last May at Johnson State College in Johnson, Vermont. One of our agents was there, of course, and sent in copies of the artists' statements of — well, of *something*, no doubt, but of what, it's hard to say. Mostly they identified the signifiers as practiced eliminators of the signified.

The most practiced is probably a certain James Welling. He is serious. He doesn't even put quotation marks around "work." He doesn't *do* works anyway. He seeks productions. Here is part of a production he found:

My work challenges the photographic ethos wherein the camera witnesses mundane details of appearance. I seek a photographic production which evokes as much as it reveals, and which resists the intelligence as long as possible. To shear the photograph of representational references produces an image of multivalent significances.

That, at least, settles an old controversy in one special case. One picture that resists the intelligence is worth forty-eight words that do likewise. So art *does* instruct and delight after all!

[VI:7, October 1982]

Politics and the Eglinsh Language

Our civilization is decadent and our language — so the argument runs — must inevitably share in the general collapse. It follows that any struggle against the abuse of language is a sentimental archaism, like preferring candles to electric light or hansom cabs to aeroplanes. Underneath this lies the half-conscious belief that language is a natural growth and not an instrument which we shape for our own purposes.

The bottom line objection against industry-sponsored educational materials is how many more products the company will sell as a result.

The multiplicity of commodities, as Ivan Illich criticizes, induces a new kind of poverty. . . .

Though corporate-sponsored teaching materials in many subject areas are responding to the needs of a relevant curriculum, they might also be viewed as expedient and defensive public relations in vested ideologies.

WE have decided to begin memorial observances of *1984* a little bit early, since such subversive activities may not be permitted when 1984 rolls around. The epigraph above, however, is not from *1984* but from a celebrated essay, "Politics and the English Language," in which Orwell considers mendacious and mindless language far more common and insidious than the dramatic and perhaps too obviously perverted Newspeak of *1984*. The other passages, written in the Eglinsh language, are all from *Hucksterism in the Classroom: A Review of Industry Propaganda in Schools,* by one Sheila Harty. Fortunately for Sheila Harty, Orwell did not live to read this book. He would have found even "industry propaganda" less reprehensible than school Eglinsh, for industrialists, unlike "educators," have never promised to devote themselves to the life and work of the mind.

Whether Sheila Harty will ever read "Politics and the English Language" we cannot say, but it seems unlikely. She doesn't really have to, you see, for her book has already been awarded, by some other people who seem never to have read that essay, what the National Council of Teachers of Eglinsh, out of the serene presumptuousness that ignorance alone can bestow, the George Orwell Award for Distinguished Contributions to Honesty and Clarity in Public Language.

We have so far, as many readers will remember, done nothing more about the NCTE than to demonstrate its culpability in the mishap at Three Mile Island, the aborted raid into Iran, and one trifling collision of a Metroliner and a work train that didn't even kill anyone, but now it's obvious that we have to stop coddling those people. And we also notice that this weird award comes, to be precise, from the NCTE's Committee on Public Doublespeak, an especially shifty bunch. They're the ones who smugly hand out brickbats for the silly and devious language of businessmen, bureaucrats, politicos, and Pentagon spokespersons (which term the NCTE approves), but never seem to notice the inane cant of the educationists or even the trendy jargon of Eglinsh teachering. They wax mighty wroth at "enhanced radiation devices," but they'll not drum out of the corps those experts "thoroughly trained in grammar, usage, and linguistics," who tell us, in their report on the Third National Writing Assessment:

While there may be a sense of sections within the piece of writing, the sheer number and variety of cohesion strategies bind the details and sections into a wholeness.

In "Politics and the English Language," Orwell cites and discusses examples of the "slovenly . . . language that makes it easier for us to have foolish thoughts." Grim as Orwell's vision for the future was, he never dreamed that we would one day actually have to worry about gross and obvious solecisms in the public language of supposedly educated people. The faults in his examples do not include such grammatical gaucheries as "bottom line is how" or the pathetic baffled-freshman-trying-to-sound-fancy "as Ivan Illich criticizes."* But even without such crudities, Harty's prose displays all the perversions of language that Orwell named: avoidable ugliness, staleness of imagery, and lack of precision.

Orwell was more specific. He discussed the routine use of the dying metaphor, that involuntary verbal twitch that tells us "that the writer is not interested in what he is saying." That seems at first an unlikely charge, especially in polemic writing, but *having an interest* in a cause is not the same thing as being interested in what you are saying. It is exactly the former that *does* lead to the thoughtless recitation of cant and stock phrases; it is the latter that demands thoughtful attention. Was it out of thoughtful attention that Harty *chose* to characterize an otherwise unspecified attribute as "responding to needs," or was it out

---

*Poor Orwell assumed, naturally, that *that* sort of language was not the problem and would never get past editors anyway. He could never have guessed that whole generations of editors (and countless other innocents) would be taught, by the NCTE and allied forces, that a persnickety preoccupation with accuracy is an elitist device for the repression of democratic virtues like self-esteem and creativity.

of her own habitual responding to the stimulus of conventional educationistic jargon? Was it after a judicious consideration of alternatives or after a jerk of the knee that she decided to distinguish one certain objection from all others by describing it as "the bottom line objection"?*

It was not out of skillful attentiveness but out of its opposite, routine thoughtlessness, that Harty ended up with "bottom line" at all, placidly content, apparently, with a particularly inappropriate jargon term borrowed from the enemy. It is out of that same thoughtlessness that the authors of Orwell's bad examples litter their prose with terms "almost completely lacking in meaning [and that] do not point to any discoverable object, but are hardly ever expected to do so by the reader." Harty would know, if she bothered to think about it at all, that her readers would accept "relevant curriculum" and even "vested ideologies" just as uncritically as she does.

Enough. You can do the rest of this yourself. Reread Orwell's essay. Even in those tiny fragments of Sheila Harty's prose, you will easily find all the items listed in Orwell's "catalogue of swindles and perversions." We have to get on with frying the *big* fish, the one who gives out prizes in Orwell's name for such rubbish.

Before it was catapulted into national prominence by being mentioned in THE UNDERGROUND GRAMMARIAN, the National Council of Teachers of Eglinsh was an obscure special interest lobbying club (a vested ideology, if you prefer). Its one little claim to fame arose, strange to

---

*Does she *mean* to say, as her garbled syntax suggests — "the bottom line objection . . . is how many more products the company will sell" — that increased sales are the *worst possible* result of "industry propaganda" in the schools? You would think that a pack of Eglinsh teachers, most of whom live on money taken from taxpayers, would favor flourishing industries and a vigorous economy. You might even think that the same people, who are devoted, of course, to the intellectual life and the freedom of the mind, might fear some even graver (or *bottomer* line) consequences of propaganda — *any* propaganda — in the classroom.

say, from what had to be either ignorance or a deliberate rejection of Orwell's most important assertion about language. Where Orwell thought language not "a natural growth" but "an instrument which we shape for our own purposes," the NCTE, in a time of troubles, made political points for itself (coincidentally taking its members off a hook and reducing their workloads at the same time) by announcing that every student had a right to a language of his own. Thus, to require of students the spelling, punctuation, grammar, and syntax of the "ruling class" was to deprive them of their rights.

Such logic would not have delighted Orwell. It finds the language of the student a "natural growth," like acne, and then proposes to protect him from the oppressive demands of conventional English because language is an instrument shaped for some purpose.

But that doesn't trouble the NCTE. What, after all, is logic? Just another tricky instrument contrived out of language. They don't care about Sheila Harty's prose, which reveals nothing more than the state of her mind; they love her *sentiments,* which show that her heart is in the right (which is to say "left") place.

Well, they may be sorry. Those greedy merchants may just this once put principle before profit and cut off the free supply of charts and filmstrips and brochures, and millions of teachers all over America will find themselves desperately trying to figure out what a teacher deprived of teaching materials is supposed to *do* in a classroom.

[V:4, April 1981]

X

The Political
Worth of Ignorance

The Answering of Kautski

Why should we bother to reply to Kautski? He would reply to us, and we would have to reply to his reply. There's no end to that. It will be quite enough for us to announce that Kautski is a traitor to the working class, and everyone will understand everything.

— Lenin

TYRANNY is always and everywhere the same, while freedom is always various. The well and truly enslaved are dependable; we know what they will say and think and do. The free are quirky. Tyrannies may be overt and violent or covert and insidious, but they all require the same thing, a subject population in which the power of the word is dulled and, thus, the power of thought occluded and the power of deed brought low. That's why Lenin's bolshevism and American educationism have so much in common.

"Give me four years to teach the children," said Lenin, "and the seed I have sown will never be uprooted." He wasn't talking about reading, writing, and arithmetic. He wanted only enough of such skills so that the workers could puzzle out their quotas and so that a housebroken bureaucracy could get on with the business of rural electrification. Our educationists call it basic minimum competency, and they hope that we'll settle for it as soon as they can cook up some way of convincing us that they can provide it. For Lenin, as for our educationists, to "teach the children" is to "adjust" them into some ideology.

Lenin understood the power of that ready refuge from logical thought that is called in our schools the "affective domain," the amiable Never-never Land of the half-baked, to whom anything they name "humanistic" is permitted, and of whom skillful scholarship and large knowledge are not required. Lenin approved the "teaching" of values and the display, with appropriate captions, of socially acceptable "role models." He knew all too well the worth of behavior modification. He knew that indoctrination in "citizenship" is safer than the study of history, and that a familiarity with literature is not conducive to the wholehearted pursuit of career objectives in the real-life situation, or arena.

On the other hand, Lenin knew that there was little risk that coherent thought would erupt in minds besieged by endless prattle about the clarification of values. He knew that reiterated slogans can dull even a good mind into a stupor out of which it will never arise to overthrow the slogan-makers. In this, our educationists have followed him assiduously, justifying every new crime against freedom of language and thought by mouthing empty slogans about "quality education."

"Most of the people," Lenin wrote, not in public, of course, but in a letter, "just aren't capable of thinking. The best they can do is learn the words." If that reminds you of those bleating sheep in *Animal Farm*, try to forget them, and think instead of the lowing herds of pitiable teacher-trainees, many of whom began with good intentions and even with brains, singing for their certificates dull dirges of interpersonal interaction outcomes enhancement and of change-agent skills developed in time-action line. Lenin's contempt was reserved for the masses. These educationists, pretenders to egalitarianism, hold even their own students in contempt, offering them nothing but words.

If you think it too rash to charge our educationists even

as unwitting agents of tyranny and thought control, consider these lines from a recent proclamation of the Association of California School Administrators:

"Parent choice" proceeds from the belief that the purpose of education is to provide individual students with an education. In fact, educating the individual is but a means to the true end of education, which is to create a viable social order to which individuals contribute and by which they are sustained. "Family choice" is, therefore, basically selfish and anti-social in that it focuses on the "wants" of a single family rather than the "needs" of society.

So what do you think? Would it suit Lenin?

And if you'd like to object, you'll see that these people also know how to answer Kautski. They'll just pronounce you an elitist, and everybody will understand everything.

[III:8, November 1979]

The Lower Strings Subcommittee
of the
ANTI-ELITISM LEAGUE

The Necks and Minds of the People

THIS month in Belgrade, the United Nations Educational, Scientific and Cultural Organization will meet to blather about the report of its commission on "the news media." That report suggests, among other outrages, that the press ought to promote, and perhaps ought to be *required* to promote, the "social, cultural, economic and political goals set by governments." We're not the least bit surprised. That's exactly the kind of idea you can expect from an outfit calling itself "educational."

"Education" once meant liberation, a condition available to those led forth (*educati*) out of some restraint or captivity. We once assumed that ignorance and unreason, although natural, were fetters that might be broken through the accumulation of knowledge and the practice of logical thought. We imagined that this trap of reflexive twitches might be transformed into the examined life.

Now it is otherwise, and "education" can be best understood as an inoculation, which, if it takes, will protect you from something much worse: *re*education. But it usually takes. Where once a tyrant had to wish that his subjects had but one common neck that he might strangle them all at once, all he has to do now is to "educate the people" so that they will have but one common mind to delude.

Even in its less malevolent forms, education has become a process intended not to increase knowledge and foster thought but to engender feelings. Sellers see no absurdity in claiming to "educate" buyers. Politicians are eager to "educate" voters. And our schools have taken up institutionalized apologetics in the cause of values clarification and social adjustment through consciousness raising. In short, American public education is *exactly* what UNESCO wants us to promote, one of those "social, cultural, economic and political goals set by government." We will decline.

We hear noises from educationists, and especially from unionists in education, about the "duty" of the press to stop knocking and start boosting, by running, perhaps, some cheery articles about boldly innovative (relevant) bulletin boards and the latest test scores, which *may* suggest that many eleventh graders are now only *three* years behind in reading. Now is the time, we hear, to "restore public confidence in the schools." That invitation is the same as UNESCO's, and, considering its source, nakedly self-serving as *well* as ominous. Again, we decline.

Public education, no less than the Marine Corps or the Internal Revenue Service, is a creature of government and an instrument of its policies. Its meager remnant of "civilian control," the elected school board, has been effectively disenfranchised by the mandates of government, which leave little uncontrolled. Public education serves one master, and that master is rich and powerful. Those who clamor for the restoration of confidence in the public schools can, with the mighty resources at their disposal, and not money alone, but the power and prestige of officialdom, easily provide that for themselves. They can easily "educate the public" into warm feelings of respect for the schools, especially since those whose values stand in need of clarification are mostly victims of the schools, unskilled in thought and poor in knowledge.

When they do that — indeed, *as* they do that, for they are always at it in one way or another — it is only the press that can put weights in the other pan of the scale, citing facts and exploring meanings.

"The functionaries of every government," wrote Jefferson, "have propensities to command at will the liberty and property of their constituents." Is that any less true when the "functionaries of government" just happen to be bureaucrats in some department of "education"? Have they not commanded our property, in countless billions, only to squander it on fads and gimmicks and nonsensical "research" and lucrative consultancies for others of their tribe? Have they not commanded our liberty and our very persons in the cause of ideological adjustment? How long would we bear such intrusive and manipulative behavior in other functionaries of government, in the Coast Guard, for example, or the Motor Vehicle Bureau?

How long? Only so long as we remain ignorant of what they are doing and thoughtlessly uncritical about its meaning. Jefferson went on:

There is no safe deposit for them [liberty and property] but with the people themselves; nor can they be safe with them without information. Where the press is free, and every man able to read, all is secure.

It is noteworthy that the people who want the press to promote the schools, thus mitigating the first of Jefferson's conditions for the security of all, are the very ones who have so egregiously failed to provide the second: universal literacy.

On the other hand, of course, Lenin opposed freedom of the press. Why, he asked, should government that is "doing what it believes is right allow itself to be criticized?" *His* values were clarified.

[IV:6, September 1980]

Nox quondam, nox futura!

Students do not read, write and do arithmetic as well as they used to because they can get along quite nicely without these skills. . . . Americans are finding that they need to rely less and less on "basic skills" to find out what they want to know and what they want to do. Our basic skills are declining precisely because we need them less.
— Peter Wagschal, Futurist, University of Massachusetts

Y EAH. And that's not all! Just you take a good look at the standard American dogs and cats. They live pretty damn well, toiling not, neither spinning, and they've never even *heard* of stuff like reading, writing, and arithmetic. They "do quite nicely without those skills," and so do tropical fish and baboons. And so, too, did black slaves and Russian serfs, and all those marvelously skillful and industrious ancestors of us all who gathered nuts and roots and killed small rodents with sticks. They all knew everything they needed to know.

We would probably never have heard of Peter Wagschal, or of his neato Ouija Board Studies Program, if it hadn't been for one Larry Zenke, a pretty neato guy himself. Zenke is Superintendent of Schools in Tulsa, Oklahoma, where men are still men. Did he quail when the national achievement test scores, which used to be quite good in that prosperous and orderly city, hit new lows last fall? Nosirree. When taxpayers grumbled, did he ignominiously promise to do better? And when the *Tulsa Tribune* started shooting off its editorial mouth about "fads" and "anti-academic garbage," did Zenke tiptoe away into the piloting of experiential remediation enhancement parameters?

No way. Not in Oklahoma. In the finest frontier fashion, he stood up tall in the middle of Main Street at high noon and told the unruly rabble that maybe they'd like to talk it over, before doing anything hasty, with his pal, Pete (The Persuader) Wagschal, who somehow just happened to drift into town. True grit.

Then, having (by proxy) brought light to the benighted fuddy-duddies of Tulsa, Zenke, who obviously knows more than he lets on, laid a little groundwork for the defense of *next* year's test scores: "Wagschal even suggests that 50 years from now we could be the smartest, most knowledgeable society that has ever existed, *and yet be largely illiterate.*"

The italics are Zenke's, not ours, and we're grateful for them. We have often wondered what kind of an idea it would take to make a school superintendent excited about the life of the intellect.

And a dandy idea it is, especially for all those much misunderstood "educators," saddled (for now) with the thankless (and difficult) task of teaching what no one will need to know when the bright age dawns. All that burnout and stress! And for what? For nothing more than an arcane and elitist social grace no more necessary in a truly "knowledgeable society" than the ability to play polo, or the lute.

And how, you ask, will people who are "largely illiterate" come to amass all that knowledge? Well, don't you worry, bless your heart. Someone will probably be quite willing to tell them what to know, even if it means all the trouble and expense of attaching loudspeakers to every lamp-post in America.

The teachers, then, will be liberated to do what the teacher academies train them to do. Zenke foretells:

Teachers, for example, will no longer be disseminators of cognitive information — machines will do that. Teachers will be program developers and/or facilitators of group membership, helping students develop interaction skills. Some educators, of course, will be found too rigid to survive this metamorphosis, but those who do will find excitement and fulfillment in their new "teaching roles."

And that will be just dandy too. Happy, happy, the teachers of tomorrow, at long last fulfilled and excited! Freed forever from the stern constraints of the tiny smatterings of mere information still incongruously expected of teachers, the facilitator-trainees of the future won't have to take *any* of those dull and irrelevant "subjects" that now impede their growth as *professionals* and their group membership development. They'll be able to spend *all* their time in the enhancement of their interaction skills, so that they can go forth and facilitate the same for little children. (Those cunning tots, of course, *do* have to be *educated*, you know, so that they will sit quietly in organized groups when it's time to hear some knowledge from the loudspeaker.) And the training program for superintendents of schools will be even more exciting and fulfilling. There's just no counting the skills that *they* can get along nicely without.

Which is it you've lost, Tulsans, your spirit or your minds? Could it be both? Do you lie awake in the still watches of the night worrying about those godless communists who are panting to nationalize oil? Do you fear that bleeding hearts will take away the guns by which you fancy that you won and may yet preserve your liberty? Pooh, Tulsans, pooh.

The most dangerous threat to your liberty, the one that

has by far the best chance of turning you all into docile clods, is right there in Tulsa. Think, dammit! Do you imagine that foreign enemies of this nation could devise for your children a more hideous and revolting destiny than the one so blithely envisioned — and as an *exoneration*, no less — by the superintendent of schools? Do you yawn and turn to the sports section, citizens of Tulsa, when the man whom you have hired to oversee the growth of understanding and judgment in your children airily tells you that in a palmier day they will have no need of the literacy that alone can give those powers? Do you shrug when he tells you that the children will be spared the burden of whatever "cognitive information" they don't actually need, which must obviously, since the children will have no powers of judgment, be chosen by someone like Zenke? Do you, like Zenke, dream of the day when no one will be able to *read* our Constitution, but it won't matter, because the machines provided by the government schools will tell us all we really need to know about it? Can you think of something to say to those teachers, and superintendents, who are *not* excited and fulfilled with leading young minds into the ways of understanding and thoughtful discretion, and who are *un*rigid enough, flaccid and limp enough, not only to survive but to hail as liberation their metamorphosis into developers and facilitators? Does it not occur to you that the inculcation of "interaction skills" for the purpose of "group development" is exactly the opposite of an education, by which a mind can find its way *out* of group-think and the pet promulgations of collectivisms? And in short, Tulsans, what are those strange black boxes we see on *your* lamp-posts? What soothing message have they recited, even as you slept? How is it, O Pioneers, that you are not mad as hell?

Oklahoma is much changed, but the descendants of the settlers still like to watch the hawk making lazy circles in the sky. Their bird-lore, however, is not what it was. In fact, there's hardly a damn one of them that can tell a hawk from a vulture nowadays.

[VI:1, January 1982]

The Children of Perez

WE were sitting around minding our own business, thinking of bilingual education and the perpetual preservation of absolutely everyone's cultural heritage, however loathsome, when the *New York Times* suddenly told us about Demetrio Perez, Jr., a Cuban émigré who has become a City Commissioner in Miami.

Perez is mad as hell because Martin Bregman, who produced *Serpico*, intends to make a movie about a Cuban émigré who makes it big in Miami as a drug peddler. From one side of his mouth, Perez says that this will "reflect badly" on Cubans, but the other side is not interested in Cubanity; *it* says that the movie would be dandy if the drug peddler were a *communist* Cuban. (Perez would also settle for a Jewish drug peddler, since he makes no objection to the fact that there are many such in the same movie.) And furthermore, Perez didn't like *Serpico* either. He says that "it tried to affect the credibility of the New York City Police Department." Accordingly, he has drawn up a draft resolution that would keep Bregman from filming his movie in sun-drenched Miami.

This is what we wonder: Does the political philosophy of Demetrio Perez, Jr., flow from the values inherent in a "cultural heritage" that our *own* government is busily doing all that it can to *preserve* in the schools, or is the man just some kind of a fool who has not *thought* about what he said? We had better hope the latter; the former promises the death of the Republic.

In either case, we'd like to send a message to Perez. Here it is:

Remember always, Perez, that it was from *that* land to *this* that you fled, whatever your reasons. And that you found this land worth fleeing to tells us something about *that* cultural heritage and *this* one. Few flee from this to that, Perez. Few flee *into* societies built on long ages of obedience to traditional orthodoxy and humble respect for authority, societies where *some* factions are *not* subject to being "badly reflected" upon, where no one would even *try* — for it is the very *trying*, successful or not, that you have condemned — to fool around with the credibility of the police, and where movie-makers do exactly as they are told by city commissioners.

In the cultural heritage that you chose not to leave behind at the border, it has indeed always been true that some people are protected, and by law as well as by custom, not only from injury but even offense. So it is that you seek for *some* people, policemen and non-communist Cubans, special protection, which must place special restrictions on *all other* people. That arrangement is abhorrent to *our* cultural heritage, in which "it is our Right, it is our Duty" to oppose with measures far sterner than offense *any* who would institute it among us.

And that means *you*.

The founders of this Republic, one of whom wrote the words you didn't recognize, were not ignorant of the political theories implicit in *your* cultural heritage. They knew them well, all too well. And they despised them and rejected them utterly. And they gave us, confirmed us *in*, a heritage that flows not, like yours, from Canossa, but from

251

Runnymede. And that was damned lucky for you, Perez.

You are probably not vicious, but only ignorant, to propose *for us* the very political principles by which *one* gang of tyrants came to oust another in Cuba. The perpetual recurrence of usurpation and counter-usurpation does seem embedded in that cultural heritage of yours, doesn't it? And if it is not embedded in *ours*, if we have not suffered the bloody grand right-and-left of princes, priests, and proles panting after privilege, there must be a reason. You could come to know and understand that reason, Perez, and you should. It is your Duty.

We welcome *you* to this land, but you can't bring Cuba, neither your Cuba nor anyone else's. Now that you are *one of us*, and by choice, it is *our* cultural heritage, in which the preservation of a movie-maker's *Right* is a city commissioner's *Duty,* that you must struggle to defend.

Frankly, Perez, we do not expect you to understand this message. But we hope you'll try, if only for the sake of your children, and *their* children. For the day may well come, through the sheer force of numbers combined with the corrosive labors of our sycophantic educationists, when *your* cultural heritage will outweigh ours. In that happy day, *your* dreams will be fulfilled. No one will try to "affect the credibility" of the police. Movie-makers will obey city commissioners.

And in that day, Perez, to what new land will your children flee?

[VI:7, October 1982]

...And furthermore

WE had fewer testy responses than expected to "The Children of Perez." Two readers wrote to say that such matters were beyond the scope (and they may have meant beyond the understanding as well) of this journal.

But the dangerous doctrines of a Perez, and the ideology out of which they flow, are protected from critical analysis in our schools, which think it good to persuade all the children into an undiscriminating "appreciation" of all known cultural heritages and "alternative lifestyles," without consideration of their implicit principles or lack of them. We approach that time when the educationists' already traditional neglect of "mere facts" like the provisions of our Constitution will be justified anew by the fact — which they *won't* call "mere" — that somebody might be offended by those provisions. As Perez now *is*.

Such a concern is *not* "beyond our scope," whatever that may be. Nor is it beyond *anyone's* scope. And that brings us to "understanding."

The search for understanding is *the* purpose of the critical examination of language. A scrupulous attention to mechanics and convention is only a paltry fussiness *unless* it reveals how and why those who seek admission to the greater mysteries will advance all the better through practice in the lesser. We want the schools to teach the skills of language *not* because that will make the students more genteel, but because it just might make them more thoughtful, and thus more likely to recognize and repudiate public displays of ignorance and unreason. Such displays, often further tainted by pandering mendacity, are the very substance of our politics and the chief agents of mindless factionalism. We are not going to wait until our Perezes dangle their participles. Their *words* are enough. To inquire into them *is* our right and duty. And yours, too.

[VI:8, November 1982]

Joanne the Jack-Killer

or, the Giant's Jolly Christmas

WE really wanted, at this festive time of year, to don our gay apparel; but it turns out that you can't do that anymore without being mistaken for a consciousness-raising band of role-players cheerily relating to an alternative lifestyle. So we decided simply to wish for peace on earth to men of good will. That proved wrong too, so we changed it to *persons* of good will. And even *that* proved wrong, for it was sure to offend a substantial and much maligned minority which should be appreciated and related to rather than demeaned by exclusion from our prayers.

It was a certain Joanne Greenberg who reminded us, and just in time, that persons of *ill will* have feelings too, you know. And rights.

Greenberg seems to be, a bit to our surprise, we must admit, the author of *Jack and the Beanstalk*. Really. It says so right here in this nifty brochure from West Publishing Company Inc., in Mineola, New York. It says, too, that Greenberg has written thirty *other* "instructional materials." This, her latest material, is not actually *called* a book in the brochure, but it is obviously meant to look like one, and it costs $5.75, a bit steep for a material. But it surely is "instructional."

It's not easy to make children hate reading stories, but this Greenberg is a *professional*. Here's how she does it:

255

Jack and the Beanstalk, by Joanne Greenberg, provides a familiar framework which allows elementary students to practice decision making while learning the basic principles of our legal system relating to fairness and honesty. The suggested activities encourage students to explore their own opinions about fairness.

Doesn't that sound like fun? How many "opinions about fairness" do the cunning little tykes *have?* Are many *against* it? Will they be set right by a merry bout of decision making? Will the teachers' manual that comes with this material teach the *teachers* those "basic principles of our legal system relating to fairness and honesty"?

But this is more than a pre-pre-law material. It is "relevant and motivating reading matter":

The activities in each chapter not only motivate the students to think critically, view situations from various perspectives, and form conclusions, but also apply language art skills such as spelling, handwriting, and creative writing.

Just imagine. There you sit, reading a book, dwelling awhile in a world strangely truer than the world, and at the end of every chapter, along comes this meddlesome schoolteacher who makes you practice decision making and "learn" legal principles. You have just watched Huck hastily covering the dead face of his friend, and this busybody, whose own "opinions" are slogans left over from teacher-school courses in interpersonal relating and values clarification workshops, calls a rap session to help *you* explore *your* opinions. Emma is stuffing her mouth with the poisonous powder, and some officious employee of the state, whose mouth drips the cant of life adjustment and behavior modification in the affective domain, "motivates" you "to view situations from various perspectives," and then to "apply" spelling.

And when Jack lays his axe to the root of the beanstalk,

will this Joanne Greenberg come barging in with her explorations and activities and maybe a neat ecological-awareness message from Smoky the Bear? Well, no. She comes up with something worse:

> One major change has been made: the Giant is not killed in the end, to avoid a violent act which would have no bearing on the issues being examined.

These school people hate literature. It stands for everything that they stand against. A work of literature comes from one, solitary mind, not from the consensus of a collective. It is an unequivocal assertion that *this is so*. It abides, or it dies, but it will not negotiate. It comes before us neither as a supplicant nor a defendant, but as a judge. It cares nothing for our favorite notions or our self-esteem. And it offends in us what most deserves offense — petulant sectarian touchiness, facile social supposition, and especially smug self-righteousness. Thus it is that the educationists' literature is not the real thing. They must abbreviate it, or amend it, or — and this is their usual practice — elucidate it, lest their students fail to appreciate correctly its relevance to "the issues being examined." And should the work at hand have nothing to do with the issues they *want* to examine, they must concoct an "instructional material" and *call* it *Jack and the Beanstalk*.

Little children know, even blithering idiots know — except for one tribe — that the Giant *must die*. The story is about the Good and the Bad, which, in the outer world of the social order, must be always cutting deals. That sad necessity *is* sad; it is *not* to our credit. When we forget to be ashamed of that compromise, when we ordain it as a principle of the inner life of the mind, when we learn to flatter ourselves for the "liberality" out of which we tolerate the intolerable, and the "flexibility" with which we gladly bend to every gust of popular novelty, then we aren't even cutting any deals. We are simply capitulating.

Jack does not capitulate. Nor does he cut a deal by accepting, instead of justice, an "enhanced interpersonal relationship" with brutal greed. He does not "view the situation from various perspectives," but seizes what is truly his, not by "the basic principles of our legal system relating to fairness and honesty," whatever the murky notions intended by that awkward phrasing, but by the one deepest principle of Lawfulness itself. And it is Unlawfulness that dies with the Giant.

And Tyranny, too, dies with the Giant, for that is another of the many names of Unlawfulness. That is why children are not frightened by the death of a brutal monster. They *know* Tyranny when they see it, for they see it regularly. It is the continued *life* of the monster, watching and waiting, that frightens them.

Children are little, and cannot live by their own efforts. They need order and principle in the world, lest they perish, in one way or another. When they find their destinies in the hands of unruly and self-indulgent parents, and teachers so unprincipled that they think it "humanistic" to "view" greed and force "from various perspectives" they recognize the Giant. While the Tyrant lives, how can they live? Must they always cut the same old deal, remake themselves after the Giant's image and likeness, lest he sniff out foreign blood in *them?* Will no one save them? Who can stand, when even the grown-ups prissily reject "a violent act which would have no bearing on the issues," against strong tyranny?

Jack — that's who.

"One cannot understand the least thing about modern civilization," said George Bernanos, "if one does not first realize that it is a universal conspiracy to destroy the inner life." Greenberg's revision is surely one of those least things, although probably an involuntary ideological twitch rather than a deliberately conspiratorial deed. She is simply "staying in line," which is the first and great commandment of all collectivisms. And the second is like unto it: Keep thy neighbor in line.

And if we send the Giant to the *head* of the line, maybe he'll be nice to us.

[VI:9, December 1982]

The Mouths of Babes

"Everybody thinks that Russia is the bad guy. We found out that the U.S.A. is just as bad because we're doing a lot of things like they are, like making nuclear weapons, like we dropped the first bomb. . . . We got the whole thing started."

To be ignorant of what occurred before you were born is to remain always a child.

T HE second quotation is from Cicero. It is one of those sayings that lodge themselves securely in a quiet corner of the mind, only now and then nagging for attention and elucidation. The words *seem* to have the ring of truth, but what, exactly and in detail, do they mean?

Our ruminations on that question have been helped along prodigiously by the *first* quotation. It is the "work" of a thirteen-year-old schoolboy somewhere in Wisconsin. A child. A child whose teachers have apparently been admitted to the greater mysteries without having to pass through the tedious apprenticeship of the lesser. They have not taught this child much about the natural form of the sentence, but they *have* told him who "got the whole thing started."

We found this schoolboy's understanding of what happened before he was born (which must be rigorously distinguished from his *knowledge* of what happened before he was born) in a column in the *Times & World News* of Roanoke, Virginia, July 11, 1983.

The author, Harold Sugg, a journalist, suggests that the

child might have been given some knowledge before he was handed an "understanding" — knowledge about the progress and intentions of German scientists, about the well-founded fears of Einstein and other refugees, Roosevelt's perfectly prudent reaction to Einstein's letter, and Truman's dilemma, unresolved to this day, and, like any of history's "what if's," unresolvable by anything less than the mind of God.

Regular readers will easily sniff out the source of the schoolboy's "understanding." It is, of course, the "packet of materials" put out by a teachers' union, the National "Education" Association. That handy-dandy guidebook for teachers who are ignorant of what occurred before they were born was "to dispel misconceptions [specifically in junior high school children] about nuclear war and the buildup of nuclear arms." When we discussed this project last December, we wondered whether that teachers' union had come up with some new and hitherto unsuspected knowledge, or whether they would dispel misconceptions in their usual way, i.e., by modifying children into some new feelings without bothering about mere knowledge. But, of course, we didn't *really* wonder.

Now that we have some evidence as to their methods, we want to consider their enterprise from another point of view.

They did indeed proclaim that their program of mega-death education was meant to "dispel misconceptions" *in teenagers*. What can be the meaning of that curious qualification? If there were some line of argument or collection of knowledge that would in fact dispel misconceptions about nuclear war *in teenagers*, why on earth would it not have precisely the same effect on *anyone* of *any* age?

Surely, knowledge is knowledge, and reason, reason. There can hardly be several of each, severally suitable to different ages. Some persons, to be sure, and no matter what their age, still have minds so credulous and unpracticed that knowledge and reason do not touch them, but if the NEA does in fact command the knowledge and reason that would dispel misconceptions in teenagers, then it must be able to do the same for many of the rest of us.

So why are we left in darkness? Why hasn't this union, ordinarily loud in protesting its devotion to the common good, dispelled all our misconceptions and brought us, in this most critical issue, to a national consensus? Why are some of us still in confusion as to who the good and the bad guys are and who started it all?

Or, to put it in a more useful way, do you imagine that those "teachers" would dare to do in public, before an audience of educated adults, whatever it was they did to bring that little boy to his shallow and altogether pitiable "understanding" of history?

Do you suppose that the little boy's teacher *shares* his belief? If so, how does such a gullible and uninformed person get to *be* a teacher? And if not, how is such a teacher anything other than a hypocrite and a molester of children? How else are we to describe one who would take advantage of a child's natural ignorance and pliability in order to arouse in him certain feelings and beliefs that will suit the manipulator's purpose?

Perhaps, however, there is a third possibility that seems, at first, slightly less horrendous. It may well be, for such *is* the standard practice of those educationists, that the devisers of holocaust education actually admitted (to themselves, but certainly not to the rest of us) that such a study might prove, well, just a bit "advanced" for the juvenile mind to understand "correctly," and thus in need of some judicious and pedagogically practicable adjustment. After all, to bring a child of thirteen to a mature and thoughtful understanding of so large and vexed an issue might take years and years! There just isn't going to be all that time in our nifty little mini-course. We'll have to leave something out, all that science and history and politics stuff, maybe, all those confusing mere facts.

Years and years. Yes, that *is* what it takes even to *begin* to form a mature and thoughtful understanding of *any* serious human issue, years and years of finding and ordering knowledge, and rational inquiry, and living, and paying attention to living, and always, always, living under the decent government of vigilant doubt.

The whole story of our educationists can be told in miniature by the example of this "course" in the dispelling of misconceptions about a stupendously complicated issue. They are reluctant to teach those things that *can* and *should* be taught to children. They do not find that a sufficiently *professional* calling. They dream of being priests and prophets, lofty enlighteners, healers of disordered young psyches, beneficent agents of social change. Scorning skill and knowledge as "minimum," "basic," and "mere," they hustle their charges into "awarenesses," "perceptions," and "appreciations" of the Great Issues, as though such sentiments were ways of understanding. Even when they have faint inklings of the fact that it *does* take years and years to seek out mature and thoughtful understandings, they decide that children *are* children, after all, and that for *them* a childish and simplified "understanding" will be quite good enough, and surely better than none at all.

So it was, for instance, that the boy who was brought to "understand" all about nuclear war was not burdened with the study of history, which could take up a lot of time and would just confuse him. And that much is true; there is a lot of history, of which we can never know more than a little. "The well of history," Thomas Mann put it, "is very deep. Shall we not say that it is bottomless?" And so it is, as anyone who has actually studied history can testify. And that is precisely why we must study it.

The study of history is an antidote to arrogance and dogmatism, because it reminds us that even those who have great knowledge, *especially* those who have great knowledge, cannot agree. It shows us that the "good guys and bad guys" theory of history is puerile nonsense, and that we can no more understand "who started it all" than we can know what "it all" is.

But our little boy did not read history. He was instead, as educationists say, "exposed to social studies."

The hokey cant of the educationists has at least this virtue: through it they reveal, however unintentionally, what is *really* in their minds. Their routine admission of wanting to "expose" students to this or that is a way of saying that they want the children to "catch" something — an "appreciation," or an "awareness," or the most virulent infection of all, a "right response."

(A "right response," in pedagogical theory, has nothing to do with a "correct answer." The latter exists only in the merely cognitive domain, while the former floats in the affective. The correct answer, in fact, may actually *prevent* the right response, just as that little boy's right response might have been prevented had Harold Sugg been sitting in the back of the class and obstructing the dispelling of misconceptions with a few correct answers.)

The swamp of social studies is *not* deep. It is shallow, very shallow, fetid and septic. Shall we not expect that he who drinks of it will catch something? And that little boy in Wisconsin has indeed caught a "right response," for his meager understanding is clearly *the* understanding that was intended by those who "instructed" him.

So the third possibility turns out to be not less but more horrendous than the other two. The claim that some inquiries that are just too "advanced" for children to understand can be simplified or abbreviated so that children can understand what they cannot understand is arrant nonsense and rank hypocrisy. In this program of nuclear warfare education, no inquiry at all was ever intended, no search for understanding through knowledge, but only the implanting of a certain belief in the uninformed and acquiescent minds of children. In Albania, too, the educationists call that "education."

If there are issues that children cannot understand because their minds are insufficiently practiced and informed, and because they have little experience of living, then *they cannot understand* them. Nor have they *come* to understand them when they have learned to recite the opinions of redactors and simplifiers claiming to be teachers.

And when they have learned that kind of lesson often enough — how often *is* that? — they will slip easily into the condition that Cicero had in mind: lifelong childhood. Childhood is not best understood as a *time* of life, for its time is variable and indeterminate. Childhood is better understood as a *kind* of life, the kind that is simply natural to those in whom the mind is still credulous and unpracticed. Such a mind cannot seek understanding by knowledge and rational inquiry, but will readily accept and recite opinions delivered by anyone to whom credulousness grants authority. There is no point in asking, of the boy in Wisconsin: What did he know and how did he reason? The useful question would be: Whom did he heed? He heeded certain *other* children, who learned the same lesson in the same way.

This is the fact that lies at the heart of all of our troubles in "education," the fact that must ultimately defeat all attempts at reform. The children in the schools are just children, who might someday, if left unmolested, put away childish things. But the *other* people in the schools, the teachers and teacher-trainers, the educrats and theory mongers, are confirmed children. They are, indeed and alas, exactly what they claim to be — "role models." And they represent the end of that process to which schooling is the means: the subversion of knowledge and reason, stern governors, by bands of cunning babies, feelings, and beliefs.

If we can escape a nuclear calamity only through some brand of ideological indoctrination in all our children, then we might inquire as to whether we *should* escape it. But thus we will not escape; we rather make it all the more possible. Violence is an extremity of unreason, and we do not escape either unreason or violence by calling the one to save us from the other.

Nor can we hope that little children who have been dosed with unreason and praised for swallowing it will one day, by magic or luck, put on thoughtfulness and require, of any who would persuade them, knowledge and reason. If that *is* a part of the natural process of growing up, which is at least questionable, it can obviously be prevented, and by nothing more than a little modification in the affective domain and the relentless display of role models who have already been suitably modified.

And it is a great pity, for children *can* learn from other children. The very teachers that we now have could easily teach the younger children things like the skills of language and number, upon which all mature and thoughtful understanding must ultimately be founded. They could lead them into reading the words of the thoughtful, words to be stored up against need, for need will surely come. They could treat the younger children like what they truly are, inheritors of wealth beyond counting, the great record of our long struggle to understand "it all," which permits no shortcuts.

But that is to say that the smaller children might some day grow up if the bigger were to grow up today. What do you suppose the chances are?

[VII:6, October 1983]

As Maine Goes...

The South Portland Board of Education voted April 11 to introduce a new high school course, Low Level American History, starting in September 1984.

The course would be aimed at the "slow readers or non-readers at the high school," Principal Ralph Baxter told the board.

The purpose of the course, Baxter said, would be to help students achieve the necessary number of points to graduate. He said the high school already has similar low-level courses in English, math, and science, the other three subjects required for graduation.

THAT is the news from Maine, as reported in the *American Journal* of South Portland for May 4, 1983, and we have to admit that we are absolutely astonished (and impressed) by that Ralph Baxter chap. We would never have dreamed that there could be a principal so precise in his use of prepositions. "Non-readers *at* the high school," he calls them, as though they just happened to be hanging around in the halls and waiting for someone to give them diplomas.

And so they are. And they will get those diplomas sooner or later, but not, as one might idly suppose, out of the compassionate largesse of an egalitarian society. Something, to be sure, *is* handed to them on a platter, but it's just a nasty mess of gristle and grease. On commencement day, when the new graduates gratefully wag their tails and lap up the orts, the Ralph Baxters of educationism wipe their jowls and belch.

In educationistic ideology, there are at least three justifications for mind-boggling monstrosities like the courses offered in Maine. Of two, the educationists are actually aware. The third, however, can be detected only through knowledge and reason.

First, there is the body count.

Even in these days, when *everyone* ought to know better, you can find an occasional defense of the schools, usually as a filler in the neighborhood shoppers' guide. The apologist is usually a superintendent dodging flak or an assistant porseffor of education padding his list of publications, and the "arguments" are always exactly the same, always the party line. And one of them is always the body count.

By counting the bodies, an educationist can easily prove, by the logic he learned in teacher school, that the American public schools are not only better than ever, but also better than any *other* nation's schools. Never in the whole history of mankind have *so many* "achieved the necessary number of points to graduate."

And then there's the business of democracy in action. The schools *are* democracy in action. When people are denied diplomas just because they were never taught to read, all who *can* read will become elitists.

The third justification, the one of which the educationists are *possibly* not aware, is the approach of 1984. The schools have certainly done their best by fostering Doublethink and Newspeak, and rewriting history as social studies. They have managed, even without two-way television, to find out lots of neat stuff about their students' feelings and beliefs. They have not yet, however, provided the One Thing most needed for the New Day — a sufficient number of proles, those slow readers and non-readers without whom 1984 just won't be the real thing. They're working on it.

Those who imagine that American education can be "reformed" would do well to meditate *not* on more money for merit pay and computers but on a child, one child. Any one of the non-readers of South Portland will do.

Consider him. He is the victim of an injustice, deprived of the fullness of humanity, the habits and powers of rational discourse and the thoughtful consideration of meaning. And how can we *now* deal justly with him? By giving him a diploma? By denying it, adding insult to injury?

In fact, the injustice can never be undone, as though it had never befallen him. He is a crooked branch, having been badly bent as a twig. It would need wise and mighty efforts even to begin to help him to grow straight. Who will put forth those efforts? If the schools were "reformed" miraculously tomorrow, what good would that be to him? Or to hosts of others in the same plight?

In the glorious world of tomorrow, when all the high school graduates can read and reason thoughtfully, our non-reader from South Portland will still be a prole, governed, and *easily* governed, by unexamined appetites, easily engendered; led, and easily, by pandering politicians, flatterers and entertainers of every sort, and those wheedling behavior modifiers who made him not only a prole but also a prole full of self-esteem.

It is *the* goal of education to deliver us from the captivity of the unexamined life and out of the power of persuaders. Those who now offer to reform education are the persuaders themselves, the politicians of either stripe, and the social engineers now running the schools and peddling garbage like Low Level English for Non-readers, for which they have already assured the need. They imagine that education is a process for *producing* certain kinds of people for collective purposes. For the moment, they suppose that the ultimate boon of education is not the examined life but the ability to outsell the Japanese.

Our famous excellence commission meditated not on the dismal destiny of one child, but on *a nation,* "a nation at risk," at risk of *not* outselling the Japanese. It will bring forth, therefore, if anything, only a revised *nationalistic* "education," a *modernized* program of life adjustment, this time with computers. And, when the need arises, the school board in South Portland will approve Ralph Baxter's proposal for a course in Low Level Computer Science.

The nature of the injustice done long ago to our non-reader is exactly this: He was put into a system that exists not for his sake but only for the sake of the nation.

The "success" of a school system designed "for the good of the nation," as construed by the government employees who run the schools, is not to be measured by the lifelong captivity of one poor clod. Some number of such clods *is,* in fact, "for the good of the nation." They can do the scut-work and provide employment for government functionaries in social services. They will always be crying for the moon and illustrating "democracy in action" by flocking into the factions of those who most persuasively promise it. We can't have *too many,* however, lest we fail to outsell the Japanese. Ending up with just the right number is an appropriate, and quite sufficient, goal of a school system that is intended for the good of the nation. In that great cause, what does it matter that some poor clod in Maine can't lead an examined life, which is probably an overrated, and *surely* a suspiciously elitist, enterprise? He'll be all right. We'll tell him whatever it is he needs to know. And he may turn out to be a productive worker, anyway, and thus to serve the good of the nation after all.

[VII:5, September 1983]

The Children of the State

A general state education is a mere contrivance for moulding people to be exactly like one another; and the mould in which it casts them is that which pleases the predominant power in the government, whether this be a monarch, a priesthood, an aristocracy, or the majority of the existing generation. In proportion as it is efficient, it establishes a despotism over the mind, leading by natural tendency to one over the body.

— J. S. Mill

SOMETIMES our readers imagine that we go too far. Once, when we concluded that the American government school system was exactly what Lenin ordered, certain readers imagined that we had gone too far. Later, when we concluded that religious schools were in no important way different from government schools, and that what Luther ordered was even more oppressive than what Lenin ordered, certain *other* readers imagined that we had gone too far.

In fact, however, we never have the space to go far enough. Of the inane pronouncements and the sentimental mantras of educationism, we ask one question, a question that should always be asked of *any* proposition, even the most familiar, *especially* the most familiar: If *this* is true, what *else* must be true? It is a little question with a big answer. It throws a wonderful ray of clear light into sunless stews of superstition all the way from astrology to the affective domain.

To answer that question, however, is usually an exasperating chore. It's difficult enough to puzzle out exactly *what* the educationists are saying, and *why* they say it, is, therefore, all the harder to construe. Often, after having worked out the logical, and horrible, implications of their dicta, we don't know whether to indict them for vice or for folly. It is thus a rare pleasure to discover an educationist who does not leave us in doubt.

He is a certain William H. Seawell, a professor of education at the University of Virginia, a paragon of clarity, a plain speaker in whom there is no mealy-mouthing, no obliquity, no jargon at all.

"Each child," says William H. Seawell, "belongs to the state." What could be clearer?

In saying that, Seawell, who is, after all, a paid agent of the government of a state, was doing nothing more than what he is paid to do. That function is called, almost certainly by every government on the face of the earth, "Educating the People." But Seawell's forthrightness, in a matter that ordinarily puts educationists to pious pussyfooting, suggests that he is no mere time-server who is just following orders. He sounds like exactly the kind of agent that *any* government most prizes: a True Believer.

And a brave one, too. For he also said, to an audience of mere citizens, gathered to "celebrate" the opening of yet another government schoolhouse in Fort Defiance, Virginia, that the purpose of "education" is "the training of citizens for the state so the state may be perpetuated."

Although Seawell probably holds to the orthodox educationistic belief that "truth and knowledge are only relative,"* he seems to have spoken as one who knew with absolute certainty that Jefferson had left Virginia forever, and could not possibly be sitting quietly, horsewhip in hand, out in the dim back rows of the auditorium. It could only

*From Bloom's *Taxonomy* (see page 71).

be out of some such certainty — although ignorance might serve as well — that a man would dare to admit that "public schools promote civic rather than individual pursuits," and to argue *from* that, that "only public education can be used to gain a free society."

Fort Defiance, eh? Well, times have changed in Virginia. Our source, *The Staunton Leader*, a remarkably restrained newspaper, says nothing at all about the mere citizens' reaction to being educated by Seawell. We have to assume, however, that even *The Leader* would have made some brief mention of the fact if the man had been tarred and feathered and ridden out of Fort Defiance on a rail. So that probably didn't happen.

And that it didn't is witness to the efficacy of an "education" designed for the perpetuation of the state. Such an "education" must see to it that its victims are habitually inattentive to the *meaning* of the words and slogans in which they are "educated." No one, it seems, muttered any tiny dissent when Seawell overruled the Constitution and appointed unto himself and his ilk the task that many Virginians might have deemed more suitable to other hands: "We must focus on creating citizens for the good of society."

So. We are now to hold *these* truths to be self-evident: That all citizens are encumbered by the State that creates them with certain inevitable burdens, and that among these burdens are a life of involuntary servitude for the perpetuation of the State, the liberty to be required by law to learn from their Creators the worth of the civic and the nastiness of the individual, and the assiduous pursuit — and this is Seawell's parting shot — of only those pastimes deemed (by agents of government, we guess) "productive."

It is possible, of course, that hidden among the impositions of George III upon the colonies there were provisions more heinous and tyrannical than William H. Sea-well's grand design for Educating the People, but damned if we can think of any just now. And it gives us sadly to wonder.

Some eminently reasonable and well-educated men found King George's comparatively mild and unintrusive intentions nothing less than a "Design to reduce them under absolute Despotism," as a delegate from Virginia put it. But the king never claimed that he was the creator — and *owner* — of his subjects, or that their *purpose* was the perpetuation of the state. He did not require the children to attend schools in which his hired agents would persuade them as to *his* notions about the "good of society." Nevertheless — and it suddenly seems strangely unaccountable — those thoughtful men took up arms against that king. Was it for *this* that they delivered us from *that?*

The citizens of Fort Defiance probably gave Seawell, at the least, a free feed. Maybe even a plaque.

Well, not to worry. All this took place long ago, in May of 1981. By now, surely, all the *other* educationists will have vigorously dissociated themselves from Seawell's eccentric views. As soon as we hear news of his repudiation, we'll pass it right along, lest you fret about the state of the Republic.

[VII:2, March 1983]

A Lecture on Politics

The state in which the rulers are most reluctant to govern is always the best and most quietly governed; and the state in which they are most eager, the worst.

WE have heard from a faithful, but worried, reader. He is afraid that Ronald Reagan might read THE UNDERGROUND GRAMMARIAN and make use of our arguments for his own devious purposes. And we have, indeed, often argued that *good* schools, cleansed of trashy courses and parasitic functionaries, would cost less than the schools we now have.

Strangely enough, our worried reader obviously did *not* suggest at all that our arguments are *wrong;* he feared only that they might be used by a wrong person in a wrong cause. And now *we* are worried, for that fear is itself a frightening reminder of the tremendous power of factional belief over the freedom of the mind.

If an argument is sound and rational, it is sound and rational no matter who uses it. If Reagan, or some other politician, or the Devil himself, should choose to espouse sound and rational argument, we would all be better off. But that cannot happen. Politicians — and the Devil — just don't work that way.

In fact, if *any* politician were to adopt our understanding about the costs of public schooling, it could only mean that he has decided not to run. No office seeker, even should he find it true, would dare to say what we say. We do not fear, therefore, that we may provide unintended — and utterly unmerited — aid and comfort either to Ronald Reagan or to *any* of his currently numerous opponents.

What we do fear, however, is a result even worse than that. Thanks largely to that pussyfooting excellence commission report, which looks more and more like a clever ploy to precisely this end, the future of education in America may be delivered into the hands of politicians, the only people around whose influence on the life of the mind is even more baleful than that of the educationists. When the *very* last returns of the election of 1984 are finally in, they may well show that the American people have been persuaded at last not only to accept but also to approve the notion that the character of "education" should be determined in the voting booth. Nothing worse could happen to us.

Among us, the rulers are not reluctant to govern. In pursuit of office, they will bellow with the herd in broad daylight, and, in darkness, hunker down with the wolves. They prosper by persuasion and the exacerbation of factional discord. Like the educationists, they prefer to ply their trade in the misty precincts of "the affective domain," where sentiment and belief can be assigned a greater "moral" power than knowledge and reason, provided only that they be "worthy sentiment" and "right belief," to which every faction lays claim. Politicians must thus depend upon the existence of a certain number of citizens who share similar desires but who neither will nor can inquire as to whether they *should* desire what they desire. Nor do our politicians find it useful to encourage such inquiry.

All of that may be "only realistic," but if it is, it points to certain loathsome realities. It must mean, (a) that Americans have not achieved that "informed discretion" that Jefferson deemed essential to a free people, (b) that politicians profit from that lack, and (c) that, as to improvements in the hen-house security system, the foxes will have some ideas of their own.

For that is exactly what an education is — a security system that signals the intrusion of ignorance and unreason. It is education that unmasks opinion or belief parading as knowledge, and defrocks persuasion pretending to be logic. It is our defense against the tyranny of appetite and ideology, and our only path to self-knowledge and self-government. It is, in short, exactly the sovereign remedy for politics as practiced among us.

We have listened to Reagan, and we have listened to Mondale, who seems sufficiently typical of the other pack. They show no sign of knowing what they *mean* by "education." According to the faction they hope to please, they take education to be some sort of more or less practical training in something or other, or an indoctrination in somebody's favorite version of socially acceptable notions, or an incoherent muddle known as "adjustment to life." They address themselves to issues related *not* to education but only to the school business, to schools as agencies of government and bureaucratic structures. They believe, or pretend to believe, that *the solution* lies in this or that, prayer, or pay, or something.

And one of those men, or someone just like one of them, will win the presidential election of 1984, trailing behind him his promises and debts. To whom then will he turn in the great cause of excellence and the reform of schooling? Plato? Jefferson? To *anyone* who understands education as the mind's strong defense against manipulation and flattery? Will he drive out once and for all, by denying them their "monies," the clowns and charlatans of educationism who have brought us to this pass? Or will he rather prove that he "supports education" by handing those innovative thrusters *more* monies?

The educationists do claim that they run the only game in town, that they are the only real *professionals* who know all about education. And, since they are not able to detect irony, they can claim with perfectly straight faces that they are the only ones who can help us, now that we have gotten ourselves into this mess.

They lie. But politicians are realistic, and they don't care that educationists lie. They care only that the educationists be *perceived* as panting after excellence, and *that* they can manage.

We face nothing less than the ultimate test of democracy, a sterner test than war itself. The survival of *the nation* may be a necessary condition of individual freedom, but it is certainly not a sufficient condition. If "democracy" means rule by those who know best how to please the uninformed and thoughtless, which is the condition asserted, and presumably accepted, by those who excuse politicians as "realistic," then we cannot be free. We must suffer the tyranny not only of our own appetites and notions, but of the appetites and notions of any slim majority of everyone else. If we tolerate the existence of such multitudes, we cannot be free. And if we permit the politicians and the educationists to define the nature and purpose of education according to *their* appetites and notions, to say nothing of their track records, then we will ensure the existence of such multitudes. And we will never be free.

Democracy is *not* a form of government that provides freedom. That it is, is the sort of illusion easily (and conveniently) induced in the multitudes who are given pep rallies in "citizenship" rather than the disciplined study of history and politics. But democracy may well be that form of government that most liberally *permits* freedom. Even Aristotle, who had no illusions about the supposed "rightness" of multitudes in proportion to their size, was willing to grant this:

"If liberty and equality, as is thought by some, are chiefly to be found in democracy, they will be best attained when all persons alike share in the government to the utmost."

An uneducated person is simply *unable* to "share in the government." Governing is exactly what is *learned* through education. The uneducated, of whatever rank or station, do not even govern themselves, but simply obey whatever desires and beliefs they suppose to be their own. But if they cannot govern, they can certainly *rule*. And should they be reluctant to do that, some realistic politician will be delighted to set them straight.

Jefferson did not commend "informed discretion" as a graceful adornment for a lucky few. He *prescribed* it as a necessary condition for *freedom in a democracy*, for he knew that the latter does not ensure the former. And he prescribed it for "all persons alike . . . to the utmost."

Well, let's keep on looking for a bluebird. Maybe Jefferson was wrong. Maybe we *can* be "ignorant and free." Someday, maybe, we'll find out. Maybe as soon as November of 1984.

[VII:5, September 1983]

THE END.